For those interested in human behaviour, and who like crisply told anecdotes, this book is a testimony to the fact that human nature does not change. In his work as a probation officer the author has seen much of the darker side of human nature as well as amassing a store of fascinating stories.

Tragedy and comedy sit side by side in the dock.

Here the criminal justice system is laid bare with both sides of the law offered up for examination. Written from the viewpoint of someone at the meeting point between the judiciary and the criminal, we are allowed an insight into the many unusual aspects of life experienced by judge, criminal, policeman and probation officer.

Anyone involved in the judiciary, or those interested in the ironies and pitfalls of human existence should read on.

☆ ☆ ☆

J R Mott served as a probation officer for nearly twenty-five years. Both his parents were music hall artists and as a great nephew of Marie Lloyd he was brought up backstage amid many colourful characters. After Second World War service with the Royal Artillery he obtained a diploma in sociology from London University and was selected to enter the London Probation Service.

Actively engaged in the welfare of sick people, he is currently a member of the local community health council. He is married with one daughter and lives in Surrey.

PROBATION, PRISON AND PAROLE

A True Story of the Work of a Probation Officer

J.R. Mott

Foreword by
Michael Varah
Chief Probation Officer, Surrey

THB

Temple House Books
Sussex, England

Temple House Books
is an imprint of
The Book Guild Ltd

Temple House Books
25 High Street,
Lewes, Sussex.

First published 1992
First Reprinted 1993
© J.R. Mott 1992
Set in Baskerville
Typesetting by APS,
Salisbury, Wiltshire.
Printed in Great Britain by
Antony Rowe Ltd.,
Chippenham, Wiltshire.

A catalogue record for this book is
available from the British Library

ISBN 0 86332 768 0

CONTENTS

*This book is dedicated to my friends Michael Varah
and Colin West without whom it may never have been
published.*

FOREWORD

For those that are inquisitive about human behaviour or indeed intrigued as to what causes people to commit crime, then this book makes compulsive reading.

Since time immemorial crimes have been committed and the reasons for those crimes, I suspect, have not altered. The emergence of the Probation Service about 100 years ago has its roots in Victorian morality and religious fervour and the first probation officers were actually called Police Court Missionaries. Whilst much has changed since those pioneering days, the Probation Service still reflects in much of its work the importance of 'advising, assisting and befriending' those who transgress the laws. Dick Mott dedicated much of his life to work with the motley collection of people who find themselves in court charged with a wide range of offences. What makes his book unique is that the stories portrayed are taken from real life rather than worked up as fictional tales drawn from the dark theatre of his mind.

I believe that this book should be required reading for anyone considering entering our exacting profession. I would have made far fewer mistakes had I access to this compendium of experience and wisdom hard won by an officer who reflects the qualities needed not only to understand the complex world of criminal behaviour, but more importantly make a real impression on those placed under supervision.

There is growing public interest in the work of the Probation Service and this book – for the first time – opens the doors to the trials and tribulations of offenders and probation officers alike in a way which is both heart warming and often full of pathos. I defy any reader, public or professional, to put this book down having started it. It is mercifully jargon-free. What emerges from its pages is a rich kaleidoscope of human behaviour which at times triggers a range of emotions, leaving you with a feeling of respect and affection for a probation officer who refuses to accept that change is not possible if you have the wit and determination to overcome the endless obstacles placed in your way.

This book is long overdue. It is neither salacious nor patronizing. Rather it is a demonstration of the art of the possible. For those who genuinely care about the quality of justice this book represents – through the experience of one probation officer – a sense of realism and empathy for those who invariably make poor criminals but deserve our attention if they are to be encouraged to lead more constructive lives. In a sense Dick Mott speaks for us all, and I believe there are many probation officers who would feel privileged to line up with him and say he is an example for us all to follow.

Michael Varah.
Chief Probation Officer, Surrey.

PREFACE

This story takes the reader at a fast pace through the wide range of human conditions observed by the author during his life's work as a probation officer. Here, set in the probation officer's room, are to be found poverty and misfortune, intermixed with love and affection, as well as from time to time, a hint of wickedness. The tales are both sad and humorous. We are also led into the judges' chambers, where the foibles of the judiciary are gently and irreverently mocked.

However, as well as being thoroughly entertaining, Dick Mott is instructive. The thread which runs through his vignettes is the employment of his professional skills. He demonstrates how training and experience enable the probation officer to find the real cause of the problem concealed behind the behaviour – often anti-social – of his subjects.

His perceptiveness helps him first interpret and then to motivate his clients towards a solution to their difficulties. The author shows how the firm structure of the probation officer's relationship to the courts enables him to guide them through their difficulties.

This is a book which should be read by anyone interested in a career as a probation officer or social worker. It illustrates better than any text book, how vital and effective is the combination of a thorough training and a deep personal commitment to helping those in trouble.

Roger Mattingly,
Director of Social Services,
London Borough of Sutton.

INTRODUCTION

Opinion is divided when deciding upon punishment. Should it be strictly punitive? Should force be met with force? How do we make the punishment fit the crime? Should punishment be written into law with the idea that, if the penalty is severe enough, it will act as a deterrent? Or should there be a more positive objective?

Should not punishment be geared to a reformative programme for all age groups based on the premise that the best way to protect the public is to try and ensure that the criminal does not commit further offences in the realization that there is a better way of life?

Perhaps the truth is that different personalities will respond to punishment in different ways, so that there may be some merit in each of these alternatives.

The Probation Service is a reformative service and the eventual aim is to guide offenders back to a normal life. Contrary to the do-gooder image, the Probation Officer is equipped with an iron fist in a velvet glove, and this sometimes comes down heavily in the public interest. Nonetheless, although there are various courses of action open to the Probation Officer, often entailing punitive measures, the service is still designed to help clients to see the error of their ways, and it is the aim of every Probation Officer to help offenders (I hate that word!), to lead a happy and industrious life.

But it does not stop here, for there is work to be done in attending Court – every Court in England and Wales has a Probation Officer attached – providing reports to assist in sentencing, and in arranging for psychiatric reports or anything that will assist the judiciary. One of the most difficult duties is to take on the role of welfare officer in the Divorce Court or in domestic cases in a Magistrates' Court, when reports and recommendations have to be submitted about the custody of children. In addition, the supervision of ex-prisoners on parole presents varying problems and can sometimes put

11

extreme pressure on a supervising officer.

A variety of problems arise in differing proportions and are dependent upon the type of case and the individual concerned, whether it be a young person, an elderly shoplifter, somebody totally dishonest, a violent personality, or a matrimonial case involving both practical and emotional crises. Luckily for all concerned, life does have a funny side to it, and quite often, the unexpected occurs which changes the whole situation. Success comes from unexpected places, and as we are dealing with human beings, and are human ourselves, we must allow for human nature.

My reasons for writing this book are therefore twofold:

First, after working as a Probation Officer for nearly twenty-five years, I would like the general public to know that we are working on their behalf – this book describes what we do, and how we do it. Secondly, I hope that, in relating some of the more interesting – and even funny – situations potential Probation Officers or Social Workers might pick up the thread of casework which can still be practised through good relationships, sympathy and understanding. I remember one rather irate Senior Probation Officer once asked me: 'What are you going to do about this fellow?', and I replied: 'I don't know, he hasn't told me yet!'

When Pauline and Terry Morris wrote their excellent book, *Pentonville* Terry told us: 'I've been here six weeks and I still can't find out what Probation Officers do all day!' Well, it's about that!

1

SELECTION: WHY ME?

REG

I was sitting at my desk writing, when the door of my office banged open with some violence. Standing at the threshold was a young man with cap on one side, looking at me aggressively . . .

'Are you Mott?'

I returned his gaze. 'I am *Mr* Mott' I replied. I never forgot his next words . . .

'All my life I've had someone like you chasing me.'

☆   ☆   ☆

At the age of twenty, I was called up to join His Majesty's Forces in the Second World War. I had left school at the age of fourteen with no particular academic qualifications, but with a strong leaning toward football and cricket, which was to stand me in good stead during my army days. I discovered, whilst in the Royal Artillery, that I could hold my own with all those better educated than I, in all the technical subjects required of an artillery surveyor. Plotting gun positions, reading maps, meteorological reports etc., and in particular, the science of Ballistics. I left the army in January 1946 with the rank of Survey Sergeant, but, nevertheless, I was extremely conscious of the fact that I had no real educational qualifications.

I went to work at Bradbury Wilkinson Ltd, Banknote and Stamp Printers, of New Malden. It was a steady and secure job and it enabled me to play football and cricket for the firm and, at the same time, earn a quite reasonable wage.

I remained at Bradbury Wilkinson for thirteen years, and made enough money to get married in 1950, and to purchase

13

my first house, but I still had no higher education. In 1957 I enrolled at the South West London Literary Institute, and embarked on a four-year course in Sociology run by the University of London. This was to change my whole life, for it was at The Henry Thornton College, Clapham, that I met my first tutor, Miss Griselda Rowntree, M.A. We would attend lectures each week and afterwards we would assemble at the pub opposite, and carry on our discussions and arguments until closing time.

It was during one such argument about crime and punishment, that Griselda remarked to me: 'You would make a good Probation Officer'. It made me think about my whole future and I resolved to make further inquiries about the Probation Service – but first I needed to get the necessary qualifications.

I eventually made inquiries at the Home Office and I was invited to attend for a general discussion and for further information. I later realized that they also wanted to have a look at me and decide if, at this stage, I might be a suitable candidate.

I duly arrived at the office, in High Holborn I believe, and was met by a gentleman called Mr Spier. I particularly remember his penetrating blue eyes and I remember thinking that he was a very astute man indeed. Not that there is anything significant in me remembering the colour of his eyes, but that was practically all I saw of him. The reason for this was due to the fact that, having made an appointment to see me, he now found that there was not a vacant office where he could interview me. Typical of the initiative shown from time to time by Home Office officials, he took me to the billiards room, where he sat at one side of the table and I sat at the other. Here I had my first interview and I was most impressed. Mr Spier questioned me about my background and, between flicking the odd red into the centre pocket, tried to make it clear what might be expected of me, and in fact, what I might be letting myself in for. For my part, I resisted the urge to send the black down the table and into the baulk pocket because be might have thought that I was becoming over-familiar. Instead, I explained that I was the great nephew of Marie Lloyd, that my father had been a music hall artiste, and that I had been brought up literally backstage, and in the theatrical environment.

14

This in itself was an education, encountering some wonderful personalities with not a few emotional crises that occurred behind the scenes.

Then there was my army life – travel and experiences – in Northern Ireland, India, Malaya, Singapore etc.

Mr Spier asked me if I had ever actually met a Probation Officer, and I told him that I had not. Deftly flicking the pink into the top right-hand pocket, he said that he would arrange for me to call and have a chat with the local Senior Probation Officer, Harvey Miles, a gentleman who I later got to know extremely well, and to whom I will be ever grateful for recommending me for the Probation Service.

Before I left, Mr Spier asked me if I had any out of pocket expenses! I still can't make up my mind if he was joking or not. On reflection I have often wondered if all this was as lackadaisical as it had seemed, or if I had been the subject of a little applied psychology. I am inclined toward the latter. Anyway, it must have been a good interview and I have never forgotten it. Perhaps that was my first lesson.

☆ ☆ ☆

I was later invited to call and see Harvey Miles at his office at Epsom Magistrates' Court. Once again I was impressed by the welcoming manner and general atmosphere of friendliness. And again, looking back, I realized that during this friendly chat I gave Harvey a good deal of information about personal feelings, ideals and principles. It became almost a discussion about personal philosophy, and I realized that, far from being a general discussion, it was a most astute interview, and Harvey would of necessity, be reporting back to the Home Office, and what is more, would be putting forward an unbiased opinion about my capabilities and suitability for the job.

On the lighter side, as we sipped our tea, I commented on two sets of golf clubs standing in the corner behind a locker. Harvey grinned and told me that one set belonged to Jack Frost, Senior Probation Officer at The Old Bailey.

I don't think Pauline and Terry Morris ever saw them!

Later, when I was actually appearing before the final selection board, the Chairman produced a letter from his folder.

'Mr Mott, we have here a letter that we received from Mr Harvey Miles supporting your application, with a strong recommendation . . . .'

Good old Harvey!

There followed a series of interviews and discussions, and eventually, a full day at the Home Office, beginning with intelligence tests, e.g.: 'I walked into a shop and:

A. SAW
B. BOUGHT
C. HEARD

a pair of shoes'

I put *heard* a pair of shoes! Oh well.

In the afternoon we had a debate about the advisability of legalizing betting shops in England. I began to feel more at home. It turned out that, of the eight applicants present, I was the only one who had actually been into a betting shop – and lost all my money to boot. It was a good debate in which I came down on the side of legalization.

While we were discussing this, a panel of four 'examiners' were making notes.

Finally, we each had an individual interview before the Panel. It was now five thirty pm and I was the last of the eight; I doubt if I was at my best. Later, when the Morrison Report was published, it revealed that only twelve per cent of all applicants to the Probation Service were actually appointed.

Early in April 1960 I received a letter inviting me to begin full-time training in the Inner London Probation Service. I would be combining three days practical work with two days each week in service training. This was known as Direct Entry, and, understandably, it was not very popular with the National Association of Probation Officers (NAPO). Nonetheless, they made us welcome and I was duly assigned, along with another trainee, Bert Shay, on 25 April 1960, to the South Western Magistrates' Court, under the jurisdiction of a wonderful lady, Miss M.A. Roloff, Senior Probation Officer, and under the direct supervision of Harry Ward, Probation Officer, to whom I owe so much.

Harry was a canny Scot who became a great friend, and

16

guided me safely through the trials and tribulations of my initial training. I cannot resist the temptation to relate a tale about him here.

I was given my very first social enquiry report to write for the Court. It was about a young chap who had committed a very minor offence of theft. Harry suggested that I should interview the lad and then write the report, as I saw it, unaided. He would then go over it with me and make any corrections he thought to be appropriate.

I eventually produced what I regarded as a first-class report, and I presented it proudly to Harry. He got out a red pen and began to delete certain passages and add words and even sentences here and there. 'I wouldn't put that!' 'You don't need to say that!' etc., until my face was as red as the now censored report.

He eventually sat back and said: 'There, what do you think of that?'

I replied: 'It's a bloody good job I got the date right!'

I rewrote the report and duly presented it to Metropolitan Stipendiary Magistrates, Mr A.H. Glenn-Craske. I've still got it. Written in the margin are the words, 'an admirable report from a trainee officer'.

Thanks Harry . . . !

2

EARLY DAYS: MY FIRST CASES

I often feel sorry for my clients, for being what they are. I think, for example, that it is tragic that a person with only one life to lead, by their own efforts, spend half that life behind bars. Some of us must have compassion for them. This, and the ability to be objective, are two of the qualities needed by those that are involved in the destiny of people less fortunate than themselves.

In December 1960 Bert Shay and myself, as part of our training, were given the opportunity to choose an experience which could be regarded as being related to the job. We asked if we could go into Wandsworth Prison and actually sit down and eat with the prisoners. At that time neither of us had ever been in prison, except as a visitor preparing reports for remand prisoners in custody. We had no experience of the living conditions or the catering.

On 19 December we duly reported to Wandsworth Prison where we were made welcome by the staff and in particular by a senior prison officer, Mr Legge. He gave us a grand tour of the prison, and one interesting incident occurred when we were in the chapel and several prisoners came in a far door whistling and chatting amongst themselves. Suddenly they were all silent and walking in a more orderly fashion. This surprised me because they had not all seen us standing at the back. Mr Legge said: 'Did you not see the man who was leading the party draw his hand across his forehead? That was a signal to the others meaning gold braid on cap – he had actually seen me'. This was our first experience of the grapevine which exists in all prisons. We were shown over most of the prison and saw solitary cells etc., but when we asked to see the death cell we were refused permission. We were told that there would be no

18

point in that, even though it was empty at the time. At lunchtime we went into the main hall for lunch, and once again the Home Office had done its stuff.

We sat at a table with one or two inmates and we were waited on by a trustee prisoner. None of the inmates queued up for lunch that day because, we were told, you are lucky – you've come on the day that the prisoners are having their Christmas dinner. We were duly served with a very creditable meal of turkey, Christmas pudding, etc.

The men at our table were interested to know why we were there and were inclined to show off a bit as though they had suddenly become our tutors for the day.

After a very good lunch we were served with the worst cup of tea that I had ever tasted. I commented about this to the trustee and he leaned over in a confidential manner and said: 'You know why, don'cher? They're not supposed to make themselves a pot of tea in the cookhouse, so they make a pot, then dry the tea leaves and put 'em back!'

You live and learn.

☆　☆　☆

At the South Western I was fortunate to be sharing an office with Barry Swinney, M.B.E. Actually, the honour of the M.B.E. was to come later, but this extraordinary Probation Officer eventually became so honoured because of his work with alcoholics. You will never find his methods of dealing with those unfortunate people in any textbook nor could most Social Workers put such methods into operation. His personality was accepted by his superior officers as being part of his approach, and all his clients loved him. Time meant nothing to him and he cheerfully accepted the immense amount of pressure put on him by his clients. I remember him walking into the office at about nine thirty am one morning, with about six pairs of trousers. He bounded in and said: 'That bugger won't be going to the pub this morning – I've got all his trousers!' Apparently, it was Social Security day and Barry had called at the flat early to give the man's wife the opportunity of getting her shopping before her husband blew the lot at the pub. This was typical of him and his clients never thought any the less of him because of these activities.

19

A few years later he went to work at Bow Street where the Chief Metropolitan Magistrate presided. One day he sent for Barry and said: 'Mr Swinney, I have heard what the accused in the dock has to say, and I am not really satisfied. I would like you to interview him and perhaps dig a little deeper. Will you let me know at the end of the morning what you think?' Barry interviewed the man in the cells, and at the end of the morning he was, once again, brought before Sir Robert Blundell, who said: 'Well, Mr Swinney – what do you think?' Barry climbed into the witness box and said: 'You asked me to dig a little deeper, Your Worship, and I've dug up a sod!'

Even though there was never a dull moment when Barry was around, he was, nonetheless, extremely caring and probably very much underrated when it came to the deeper understanding of the problems of both his clients and their families. His unfailing maxim: 'Never – ever – trust an alcoholic', was conveyed not only to those involved with the alcoholic, such as family, friends etc., but to the man or woman in such a way as to give them a much better understanding of their own problems and the subsequent practical and emotional problems that they created for those around them.

Some months after I first met him, in conjunction with Lord Soper, he got several of us involved in the opening of a clinic for alcoholics in Regent Street. It was in the basement of the old New Gallery Cinema, which was, at that time occupied by a religious group called the Seventh Day Adventists. This group was most helpful, and we ran the clinic more or less on the lines of a pub, with tables and bar, but only tea or coffee was available. It caught on at once, and after a few months we were always crowded. We had a side room where clients could consult a doctor in private and several doctors came to visit and offer their services – mainly, I believe, to try and get some first-hand knowledge of a subject which is often baffling and frustrating.

In many ways it is a physiological problem, with the alcoholics aware of their own shortcoming, often wishing to do something about it, and then literally turning to another drink 'to drown their sorrows'. Well, it may not be quite as simple as that, but the feelings of guilt, sometimes resulting in aggression and violence, are all part of it.

One of our patients was told one day that his wife had only

twelve months to live. From that moment he stopped drinking. He and his wife came each week to the clinic and we gave them all the support that we could. He got a job, and during the next twelve months they were probably happier than they had been for a long time. Barry could see the red light, and kept very close to them until eventually the unfortunate lady died.

After the funeral, her husband went missing – we knew what he was doing but we didn't know where he was. Then – three weeks later – he appeared in court charged with being drunk and disorderly. We got him home and were able to get him back on his feet – and back to the clinic. But while he was missing Barry Swinney had gone to his house every day and fed the cat!

Sharing an office with a man like this was an education in itself. And he did give me one invaluable tip. If you wish to make an initial appointment with a person with a drink problem – meet them in the pub. One more drink won't make that much difference, and at least they'll turn up!

Sadly, the Regent Clinic for Alcoholics in Regent Street was forced to close when the New Gallery cinema was demolished, but it was the forerunner of some excellent treatment centres now in existence.

☆ ☆ ☆

One day I was in my office when the door burst open and in walked two youths, both aged seventeen, with shoulder-length hair. This was the first time that I had seen hair this length, and as I was gazing at them, one of them said: 'You the probation geezer?'

'Yes.'

'A bloke in the Court sent us round to find you.'

'Which bloke do you mean?'

'You know, the Judge geezer – he's just put us on probation for two years – he told us to come and find you.'

'Ah, you mean the Magistrate – what had you done?'

'We nicked a motorbike. We weren't gonna keep it – we just wanted to have a couple of goes each and then dump it.'

'Hm.' I surveyed them with a critical eye. 'What do you mean by coming into my office looking like Lloyd George.'

'Who??'

'Lloyd George.'

'Oo's 'e – never 'eard of the geezer.'

I looked at the second youth. 'Tell him who Lloyd George was.'

'I ain't never 'eard of the geezer neither.'

'Right,' said I. 'You can both report here to me next week, and you can both tell me who Lloyd George was, that way the first week on probation you will have learned something.'

A week later they both returned.

'Right,' I said to the first one. 'Who was Lloyd George?'

'Oh blimey, I forgot to ask me dad.'

I turned to the second one . . . 'Tell him who Lloyd George was.'

'I dunno. I thought of asking me dad, but I couldn't fink of the geezer's name.'

These two lads turned out quite well. They responded well to supervision and often asked my advice on quite a number of subjects. There was no great problem, and, after I managed to get both of them jobs, even their appearance improved – however they kept their long hair.

A whole year passed by and they called in to see me one evening for a chat – no problems.

'Where are you going at the weekend then lads?'

'Up the Granada on Sunday.'

'Oh, who's appearing there on Sunday then?'

'Wee Willie Harris.'

I looked aghast. 'Wee Willy Harris? Who's he?'

Mick looked at me with scorn . . . 'You tell us next week and you'll have learnt something!'

I really was amazed that they had remembered the content of our first meeting, and once again, I learnt something – not about Wee Willie Harris (although I did make enquiries in case they asked me), but about the impact that the initial interview can have on some clients.

I think it was these two lads who made me realize that we can all learn from our clients, particularly from those with a different way of life. After all, Wee Willie Harris meant more to them than Lloyd George meant to me! . . . what's important? Sometimes some of the more serious problems seem insurmountable; they are many and varied, and often lead to unacceptable behaviour. But sometimes, too, a little wise counselling and/or practical assistance might result in changes of behaviour patterns – hopefully for the better. Barry Swinney used to say that our first duty was to do our client no harm!

☆ ☆ ☆

In 1961 I was confirmed by the Home Office as a Probation Officer in my own right. I was justly proud because I had succeeded in my training, which was most effective and highly organized, with written examinations as well as practical work. But during that year I also passed examinations at the University of London and was now the holder of a Diploma in Sociology. I was lucky enough to gain a Certificate with Merit in Social Psychology, and I was involved in all of this in the same year. It was hard work, but looking back, I am grateful to all those, and there were many, who helped me on the way.

3

THE SOUTH WESTERN

The South Western Magistrates Court was, at that time, situated in Balham High Road in a big old converted house. The courtrooms were in a large room in the house and in a temporary building that had been erected at the rear. Most of the probation offices were upstairs, and the Clerk's office and Warrant Officer were on the ground floor. The original court at Lavender Hill, Battersea, had suffered war damage, and was being rebuilt. It was actually opened by the Quarter Sessions Judge, Henry Elam, on Friday, 17 May 1963. Until then we were obliged to suffer overcrowding etc., but we all worked together and it was a happy atmosphere.

The two stipendiary magistrates were Sir John Cameron, and Mr A.H. Glenn-Craske – affectionately known as Uncle Arthur – probably due to his friendly habit of advising all and sundry how to do their job. Sir John was a quiet, canny Scot, who was always a perfect gentleman. I often heard him say to the accused: 'I'm awfully sorry but I can't see any alternative, I'm afraid you will have to go to prison for six months.'

The accused sometimes almost thanked him!

Sir John quietly taught me a lesson that I never forgot. I had written a report in which I suggested that, after looking at the defendant's record, he might treat him leniently. Sir John asked me: 'Do you mean that he deserves six months, but I should give him four? The word, Mr Mott, is appropriately, not leniently!'

Mr Craske was described in the press as an irascible magistrate. Certainly he did not suffer fools gladly, and could be quite fearsome at times. Yet behind the scenes he was a kind and considerate man, with a great sense of humour. It was true that not everybody liked working with him, mostly because he

24

demanded a hundred per cent efficiency. Later on when the new Court had opened, it was adjacent to Lavender Hill Police Station. The Police soon found out that a good way to annoy Mr Craske was to tie stray dogs to the outside railings. The subsequent barking invariably brought forth a strong protest to the Court Police Inspector. 'Inspector, this is the only Borough in London with a dogs' home of its own, and I have to put up with that!'

I hadn't really got a decent suit to wear in Court, and I hadn't got much money to buy one. Barry Swinney, of course, knew just the place to go and buy one. 'We'll go and see George up at Hyde Park Corner. I did him a favour years ago and he always treats me well.'

The favour he did him had been to rescue him from alcoholism, put him back on his feet, get him a job as a tailor and then help him to start up his own business. Just a little favour by Barry's standards!

Now, Mr Craske had always fancied owning a Donegal Tweed overcoat, and he somehow discovered that I was going to see George to get a suit. He got Barry to include him in the party, and we went up to London, where I bought a very nice suit for £7. Mr Craske bought his Donegal Tweed coat, and everybody was satisfied. That week, I proudly wore my new suit to go on Court duty. This brought a broad grin from the Bench! At about eleven thirty am I returned to my office and had just sat down when I heard cries for help. I went outside and there found a very distressed woman. 'I think that my son is having an epileptic fit in the gents' toilet,' she cried. I went into the toilet and sure enough there was a young man showing all the symptoms of an epileptic fit. I wrapped my handkerchief around my forefinger because I knew just enough about it to try and stop the unfortunate person from biting his own tongue by pushing it back with my knuckle.

This can sometimes be a quite violent situation, and today was no exception. In addition, an over-zealous cleaner had soaked the whole flagstone floor with Jeyes Fluid. As I was attempting to assist him., the youth grabbed me, and together we collapsed on to the toilet floor. We rolled over a couple of times, and then the epileptic fit came to an end. The youth got up – brushed himself off – and after looking at me as if to say: 'What are you doing down there?' he left!

25

I got up, my new suit covered in Jeyes Fluid and other toiletries, tottered back to my office and wondered what the bloody hell I wanted a job like this for! And then the telephone rang. 'You're wanted in Court, right away.' I cleaned up as best I could and, red-faced, I went into Court. Mr Craske gazed at me for about a minute – he sniffed the air – and then announced: 'The Court will adjourn for fifteen minutes!'

Some months later a young man came into Court charged with stealing a coat from the back seat of a car that had been parked near Chelsea Bridge. He pleaded guilty and was asked by Mr Craske: 'Why did you steal that coat?'

'I'm sorry, sir, I'd been drinking and it was a cold night – I saw the coat on the car seat and when I tried the door of the car it was unlocked, so I took the coat – I'm sorry now.'

'You'll be fined £25 and in future, if you want a coat, see the Probation Officer . . . we know where to get coats, don't we, Mr Mott?' – and then with a grin – 'And Suits!'

☆ ☆ ☆

One morning Mr Craske was in an angry mood and he had just made a Probation Order to an outside Court. He called me into the witness box and snapped at me: 'What's the Petty Sessional Division of Brentford?'

'It is Brentford, sir.'

'Rubbish!'

I looked at him with a steady gaze.

'Have you looked it up?'

'No, sir.'

'Go and do it. The Court will adjourn.'

My very concerned colleague, Colette Maitland-Warne, was most upset.

'Are you going to look it up, Dick?'

'No, I'm not.'

'Well then, I am.'

A few minutes later, she returned. 'You were right – it *is* Brentford.'

When the Court reassembled I entered the witness box.

'Well?'

'Brentford, sir.'

I turned and walked straight out of Court, pausing only to

give him the customary bow.

Later that day I went to his room to get him to sign some documents. I was actually bearding the lion in his den. He signed the documents and then said: 'Look here, I'm sorry about what happened in Court this morning. You were right and I was wrong.'

I said: 'Well, I feel I owe you an apology as well, sir.'

'Not at all. It was all my fault.'

'I wanted to apologize to you for allowing you to embarrass me in Court – and I promise I'll never let you do that again.'

He looked at me and then held out his hand – we shook hands, and we never had another cross word all the time I worked with him.

I can't leave Mr Craske without relating my favourite story about him.

Two Scotland Yard detectives had been to the Oval to watch cricket, and when they came out they went down to the Oval tube station. Here they noticed a man attempting to pick pockets, and after observing him for a while, they eventually arrested him and handed him over to the local police. This happened in May, but because of more urgent duties at the Yard, it did not come to South Western until August. It was a very hot day indeed and the case had been specially arranged for three pm.

By this time Mr Craske was almost asleep. His head had sunk on to his chest, and he was breathing heavily. We were all looking at each other but nobody dared to try to wake him.

Notwithstanding this, the first rather high-powered detective briskly entered the witness box, held the Bible high in the air and announced . . . 'Detective Sergeant So and So, New Scotland Yard . . . Your Worship – this was on Thursday, 29 May . . .'

Mr Craske never moved – he didn't open his eyes – but he said: 'The 29th of May was a Friday!'

☆ ☆ ☆

The weekend before his tragic death I was on duty all day on Saturday. During the afternoon he sent the Usher to get me, and the Usher told me that he had been in a terrible mood all day. Of course, he was extremely ill, but we didn't realize it. I

27

entered Court and went into the witness box, and I became aware of an almost electric atmosphere. When I got into the witness box he announced to the Court: 'Now we'll have some commonsense!'

Under the circumstances it was one of the greatest compliments ever paid to me. Unfortunately, I never saw him again.

4

CASUAL CALLERS

In most Courts, particularly the Courts in thickly populated areas, there is a Probation Officer on duty each morning to advise or assist the general public. It is more helpful, where possible, to telephone for an appointment, but nobody is likely to be turned away if an Officer is available. The problems dealt with by the Duty Officer are many and varied. The Officer may sometimes deal with the matter personally, or may refer the client to a more appropriate agency, depending on the problem. Quite often it would seem to be more appropriate to refer the matter to a solicitor, particularly if legal representation, or advice, may be required. For many years, this has been a valuable service given by Probation Officers, and many people have been grateful for the assistance that has been given.

I think it may be true to say that the majority of cases relate to matrimonial problems. A great deal of valuable conciliatory work is done each year, but in other cases the matter may have to be resolved in the Domestic Court for the establishment of separation orders, maintenance, custody of, and access to, children, etc. Probation Officers take these cases very seriously indeed, because so much may be at stake for the future of the parties concerned – particularly the children – as I will refer to later on.

Some of these cases, however, are more easily resolved and are often most interesting. They are, of course, very worrying for the client concerned, and I often wonder what my own state of mind would be, in order to prompt me to go to the Probation office for advice.

For instance, I once went into the waiting room and there found a well-dressed, West Indian lady. I asked 'Can I help

29

you?'

'Are you a Probation Officer?'

'Yes, I am the Duty Officer today.'

She looked slightly embarrassed. 'It is quite confidential.'

'Perhaps we should go into my office – we will not be disturbed there.'

She followed me into the office and sat down.

I sat back and waited.

'It's really about my husband – I wouldn't like it to become public knowledge because he is quite well-known.'

'Well, perhaps you had better given me your name and address, and then we will begin at the beginning.'

'Yes, I am Mrs Rabathaly – I live at . . .'

I was thinking; the name did not ring a bell, but I did not interrupt.

She went on. 'My husband is a well-known boxer. He once fought Archie Moore for the world title . . . ' (now my brain was racing) '. . . we did very well, and we bought our present maisonette at Upper Tooting. He is thirty-four years of age now, Mr Mott, and they are trying to press him into one last fight. Worse still, he is considering raising money on our maisonette in order to back himself. He is a lovely man and I love him very much, but I think that he is under the influence of others. I don't think he can win, and I don't think that they think so either – in which case we are in danger of losing the money we have got – or our home.'

'You said that he fought Archie Moore for the World Title?'

She knew what I meant. 'His name is Yolande Pompey Rabathaly – he fights under the name of Yolande Pompey.'

Of course! I looked at her – 'I'm not sure what I can do to help – what had you in mind?'

'Mr Mott, he has to give up boxing and get a job – we haven't much money and I am working in a West End dress shop. He needs to be advised by somebody we can trust.'

'Will he come and see me, if I write to him?'

'I think he will. He is a very nice chap and wouldn't wish to offend you.'

We went on to have a general chat, and although I didn't know it at the time, it was the foundation of what was to become a firm friendship. I wrote a letter, by hand, inviting him to call and see me at my office the next day, and Mrs

Rabathaly took it with her.

At ten am the next morning I went into the waiting room and sitting in the corner (how appropriate!) was Yolande Pompey. He gave me a huge grin and said: 'Mr Mott?' I knew him by sight. I advanced towards him, adopting my best boxing stance, and pushed out an imaginary straight left followed by a right uppercut. He grinned even more and ducked his head as though to let me hit him – we shook hands as though we were old friends.

In the years that followed I never knew him to act aggressively or in anything other than a friendly manner. We went into the office.

He agreed that he would like to have one last fight – he just wanted to prove something to himself.

'At the risk of losing your home, and possibly your wife. If you do it and lose, she will go back to Trinidad.'

He became subdued. 'What else can I do? I haven't much money – everybody seemed to make money out of my fights except me.'

'That is just the point – what else *can* you do? What are you any good at apart from boxing?'

'Not much. I'm a good driver.'

'Well, the first thing you have to do is make a firm decision to retire, and then we'll see about the future. OK?'

He nodded thoughtfully. 'Mr Mott, my wife asked if you could call for a cup of tea tomorrow afternoon? I'm just up the road near Tooting Bec station.'

I said: 'That's great, I'd love to, and by the way, I may not be able to punch you on the nose, but I'll kick you in the balls if you sell that maisonette.'

I went to tea the next day. They sat together and were looking at each other with side glances. She poured the tea and then said, with a trace of a tear in her eye: 'Yolande has given up boxing, Mr Mott, he has now officially retired. We phoned his manager and told him this morning.'

I looked at them both . . .

'Can you come to my office tomorrow afternoon?'

The next day, with them both present, I telephoned the West Indian Federation Embassy. A young lady answered. I said: 'I want to speak to the Ambassador about Yolande Pompey.'

She said: 'I have never heard of him.'

I told her: 'On his sitting room wall he has a certificate signed by both Mr Manley and Mr Bustamante, Prime Ministers of your country, praising him for his sportsmanship.'

She said: 'Just a moment, please.'

Then a man's voice came on: 'Hello, Mr Mott, this is Leary Constantine. Of course I know Yolande Pompey – can I help?'

Yolande went to see Leary Constantine, and as a result of their meeting, several weeks later, he became the official chauffeur to the West Indies Ambassador. We remained friends for many years after that, and he combined his new job with some coaching in boxing.

Sadly he has now passed on and I believe his wife has returned to Trinidad.

☆　☆　☆

It was some years later when I was in Court at Lavender Hill, when an Old Age Pensioner, aged seventy-three, was before the Court charged with common assault. The Magistrate (Mr Craske) was told that the defendant was resident in an old people's home in Wandsworth. Unfortunately he was often aggressive and wanting to fight with other occupants of the home. This eventually came to a head when he started a fight with another resident. It was not too clear what happened, but the man in the dock was sporting a huge black eye. The Magistrate asked him why he was aggressive and he said that the other man had picked the fight.

'He started it, My Lord and I decided to finish it. He was only sixty-seven but I put him down twice!'

The home decided they had had enough and the Court was told that he could not return there. Mr Craske asked me if I could find him somewhere to live, and after several telephone calls and enquiries, I eventually persuaded a home at Streatham Vale to accept him as a resident. He was Conditionally Discharged, and I helped him to get his belongings together to take him to his new home. We climbed into my car and he told me: 'When I was champion, I had an Alvis. That was a nice car.'

I looked at him. 'Champion?'

'Yes, I beat Matt Wells for the world title.'

32

'You were world champion?'

'Yes, I beat Matt Wells.'

I still didn't know whether to believe him or not, but I was curious enough to telephone a well-known reporter, Peter Lorenzo, and ask his opinion. I am still not sure whether Joe Simmonds was actually world champion or not, but the next day there was a picture of him in the *Daily Herald*, with the caption 'The Champ's last fight' – black eye and all.

The following week I received a letter telling me that the writer had been a mate of Joe Simmonds on *HMS Lion* during the First World War. 'Please send me his present address, Mr Mott, because I would like to help him.'

I passed on the address, and later I visited Joe to see if he was all right. His friend had visited him, and Peter Lorenzo had written about him in the *Daily Herald*. Once again he was happy in his reflected glory – he was no trouble after that.

On another occasion, I walked into the waiting room at Lavender Hill to see if anybody was waiting to see a Probation Officer. It was just before lunch and not many people were about. Nobody was in the waiting room, but the window had been opened and a young man was standing outside, on the window ledge. I looked at him calmly, although I felt far from calm inside.

'What are you doing out there?'

'I'm going to jump.'

'Oh, well, do you mind if I make a suggestion?'

'What is it?'

'My office is next door – if you jump outwards things will get much worse, but if you jump inwards maybe we can sort something out – anyway, things can only get better.'

I turned round and walked out of the waiting room, leaving him on the window ledge.

Now I was really biting my nails. I grabbed the telephone and rang the Warrant Office – no reply – come on! Supposing he jumped – where would that leave me? Still no reply. Should I go back and attempt to grab him?

My initial reaction was, I realized, based on training and experience, without my even knowing it. Should I wait? There was a knock on the door. He walked in and slumped into a chair. I sat down. We looked at each other.

'Are you all right?'

He nodded.

'Shall we talk about it?'

His name was Ken. As I remember it, it was an act of despair – a definite cry for help.

When faced with the situation it is usually the case that more expertize, or appropriate treatment may be required. Whatever I did or said, there was always the danger that he would try it again – perhaps with disastrous results. It is not a question of passing the buck or avoiding one's responsibilities. But it is certainly a question of seeing that a most unfortunate individual gets the assistance or treatment that is needed. Part of the training of the Probation Officer is to diagnose the problem and refer to the appropriate quarter. I have always wondered how I would have felt if he had jumped. In retrospect there were course of action open to me, but I take consolation in the fact that he didn't jump, but that he might have done if I had done something different.

✩ ✩ ✩

REG

One day I asked Reg if he would come to my house and put a radio in my car. He came on a Sunday, and as lunchtime approached he said he would go to a local cafe for lunch. I told him that I could not allow that, and was expecting him to have lunch with me and my family. He was somewhat ill at ease, but we made him welcome and all went well until my mother (as mothers do) said: 'You seem to be a nice boy, Reg, why do you break the law?'

Reg blushed and said: 'It's all right for you, missus, you ain't never 'ad yer collar felt.'

Mother smiled and we went on eating in silence, then she leaned across to me and said: 'What does he mean?'

5

OFFENDERS

At this point I would like to tell you about a particular case that I had some years later. I'll tell you now because there are certain aspects of this case that relate to all others, and particularly to most of our clients.

The case involves a little boy, living with his mum and dad quite happily until he was twelve years old. It was then that he developed curvature of the spine, and, to put it bluntly, became a hunchback. To add to his developed misfortune, his mother died and he was eventually looked after by another lady with whom he lodged. He finished his education but a job was hard to find. He was willing but because of his illness he lacked strength, and he was of very limited ability.

When his landlady also died, he was about seventeen. He suffered an emotional breakdown and had a short spell in hospital. He was finding it very hard to accept the fact that he could not be assisted by the medical profession and would always be incapacitated by the curvature of his spine. He was becoming aggressive and anti-social, and found it difficult to make real friends. He became a loner, but he did not lack acquaintances, most of whom bought him a drink because they felt sorry for him.

One day he went into MacDonalds and tried to chat up an attractive girl of about his own age. He became aware that she and her girl friend were really laughing at him. He went down the road, picked up a brick, and threw it through a shop window. Of course, he was arrested, and was eventually made subject of a Probation Order.

There is a saying in the Probation Service: that your client chooses you. This particular client would not have chosen anybody because he had something to prove. He didn't need me, or anyone else, he could do it on his own. After all, if anybody got near enough to befriend him, they died, didn't they. And yet he wanted all those things that a normal youth of his age wanted. And why not? He told me about the girls in MacDonalds, and how they had laughed at him, and I made one of my many mistakes with him.

'Look,' I said, 'there are some very good clubs these days for disabled people, and there are some really nice and attractive girls there. True, some of them have similar problems to your own, but they can be really nice company. Why don't you let me make some inquiries and see if I can get you to join?'

He looked at me with scorn. 'What makes you think that I don't want Marilyn Monroe – same as you!'

I have said that his case was similar to many of the others. How, you may ask? They all have a problem like his haven't they? Only usually theirs are inside or invisible and unacknowledged. His was simply more obvious. As one doctor told me: – 'If we could cure his back we would change his personality and he would be a different person – but we can't.'

My job was obvious – but almost impossible. I had to get him to accept the situation as it was and to learn to live with it and make the best of it. This was easier said than done.

He acquired a broken down old van, but, of course, with no tax or insurance. At one time he used to sleep in it until the police told him he might get 'done' for being over the limit in charge of a car – and then sometimes he slept rough. I got him lodgings and for a while he was all right. One day he was driving his van when he saw an alsatian dog attack an elderly lady. He stopped and went to her assistance. On its hindlegs the dog was bigger than he was, but he managed to drag it off and eventually the police arrived. The lady was taken to hospital and he was praised by press and police alike. But he still got done for having no tax and insurance – the police had no choice.

The pressure, poverty, worry, loneliness etc., one day got the better of him, and he walked into a new car showroom and did hundreds of pounds worth of damage to the cars. He was sent to prison for six months and he went into Wormwood Scrubs on the same day as a well-known criminal came out. Perhaps even to the same cell. As his doctor once told me: 'He is one of the more unfortunate sods of this world.'

Your client chooses you! He didn't choose me, but he didn't choose to have a hunchback either! In other cases I always tried to find the root of the problem. Perhaps I might be more successful than I was with him.

☆　☆　☆

When interviewing the general public, what sometimes seems to be a rather trivial matter to the Duty Officer, may be far more serious in the mind of the caller. Sometimes the solution to the problem is so evident that one wonders why that person needs to call and ask the advice of a Probation Officer.

An example of this arose once when a lady called and told me that her husband had left her and was living with another woman. She knew he would never return, and she had no contact with him. She was now short of money, but she could cash an insurance policy if she could get his signature on it. It all seemed fairly straightforward, and she even had a telephone number where I could telephone him. She said, with tears in her eyes, that she could not bring herself to speak to him. I telephoned him and I found him to be most reasonable. He lived locally, and he agreed that if I brought the policy round, he would sign it.

This we did, and that evening he signed the policy and I dropped it in to her on my way home. All very simple, except that she burst into tears when I delivered it to her. All this happened in October, and I had forgotten all about it, but a few days before Christmas there was a tap on my door. She hurried across the room, tears in her eyes, and placed a bottle of sherry upon my desk. She didn't speak a word but, in spite of me calling to her, she ran off down the stairs. She did the same thing each Christmas for the next five years – never speaking.

I left the Court that year and never saw her again, but that bottle of sherry each year obviously meant a great deal to her.

☆　☆　☆

One morning, an elderly couple entered my office, looking very apprehensive indeed. 'Er, we don't know if you can help us. Are we in the right place?'

'Well, suppose you tell me about it, and then we'll see what we can do.'

'It's about our grandson, he's fifteen and he lives with us because his parents are divorced. His mother is our daughter, but she is living with somebody else and doesn't see him very often. We don't know where his father is now, but he never sees him.'

I waited.

'Just lately, well, during the past year, he has run away from home a couple of times. He always comes back after a few days, and we don't really know where he's been. He's a good boy really, and when he's at home he's not a bit of trouble.' She went on. 'Well, he ran away again about two weeks ago and we've been worried out of our lives because he has never stayed away as long as this before.'

The elderly gentleman reached into his pocket and produced a letter.

'We received this yesterday, Mr Mott, and we don't know what to do next – he's in France!'

'Can I read it?'

The contents of the letter were even more surprising. It was a cheerful letter telling them he had actually stowed away on a ferry and then hitch-hiked to Nice! While enjoying himself on the Riviera he had suddenly been taken ill and eventually been rushed to hospital. This letter had been written from a hospital in Nice, couched in terms that almost suggested that he was in a local hospital at home . . . 'It's all very nice, the food is good – the nurses are wonderful' etc., etc.

'Do you think you can help us, Mr Mott?'

'Well, the first thing is, have you told his mother? She is entitled to know. Is she his legal guardian?'

'Oh yes, she is, but we haven't told her because we don't want to lose him.'

'I think you must let her know; however, let's see what we can do.'

I telephoned the French Embassy in London and outlined the situation. They were very sympathetic but said that they could not do very much at this stage because he was still in France. However, there was a British Embassy office in Nice and they were kind enough to give me the telephone number.

I telephoned the British Consulate and outlined the case. The man at the other end was most helpful and took down a lot

38

of background information – 'Has he any papers? Date of Birth?, etc., etc. 'He is English, is he not?'

'Yes.'

'OK Mr Mott. I'll visit him in hospital and find out what the exact position is. I will write direct to you and you can keep his grandparents informed. Meanwhile would you mind writing to me and putting all this on paper? It will be helpful to have a complete record of the case. Tell his grandparents not to worry – we will look after him.'

And look after him he did! A couple of days later I received a letter from the Consulate. The boy is being treated for a kidney complaint. It is not serious and when he is ready to be discharged they would escort him home. He did indeed stow away on a ferry, really in a spirit of adventure. He has now been admonished by a Consular official about the trouble and anguish he has caused and is going to apologize to his grandparents. He has promised not to run away again.

I passed the good news to the old couple and they were both relieved and grateful. His mother had been informed and she blamed herself to some extent. She promised to keep in closer touch with him in future.

So all's well that ends well . . . However, four weeks later, the old couple knocked at my door – both again looking very anxious.

'We want to thank you for all you did, Mr Mott . . . But we have received a bill for more than £200 for treatment at the French Hospital. We haven't any money, Mr Mott, we are only pensioners and we can't really pay it.'

I telephoned the French Embassy in London and explained all that had taken place. 'They had received a bill for more than £200, and they really can't manage to pay it!'

Now here's a bit of information that might assist some of my poorer readers, should they be taken ill in France.

'Don't worry about it Mr Mott,' I was informed. 'In cases of genuine hardship we are prepared to write it off because French visitors to Britain often get free treatment under the National Health Service.'

☆　☆　☆

In many cases, prior to an offender being dealt with by the

Court, reports concerning background, work, income, health, etc., and anything that may be considered relevant to the case, may be requested by the Bench. In some cases there is a statutory obligation to provide such reports, but the Court may feel that they would be helpful, and that information additional to that already given in evidence or by any other interested party would assist in arriving at a just decision.

The Probation Officer is an officer of the Court, and when acting in this role it is essential that the person concerned is seen as such. When judges or magistrates have a feeling of confidence and trust in their Probation Officers, the recommendations contained in the social inquiry report are usually taken as being reliable and safe to act upon, should the Court follow the recommendations of the Probation Officer.

Judges and magistrates have an extremely responsible job to do, and they, judges in particular, will not share the burden of responsibility lightly. In this sense, the role of the Probation Officer is of the utmost importance, and should be regarded as every bit as responsible, both to the Court and the client. In many cases, the decision of the Court has far-reaching effects, not only upon an individual but quite often upon members of the family.

The unexpected sometimes has quite a bearing upon the situation when seeking background information. Lord Denning has been quoted as saying that the dignity of the Court must be maintained at all times. I am old-fashioned enough to believe that Court officials should look, and behave like Court officials, and I agree with Lord Denning that the manner in which British Courts conduct themselves plays an integral part in the administration of justice.

A young man appeared at the South Western Magistrates Court charged with breaking and entering and theft. He was an absolute 'hippy', with torn jeans, hair all over the place, beads round his neck and a ring in his ear.

And yet, when he pleaded guilty to the charges he appeared to be well-mannered, well-spoken and polite. His parents were apparently very nice, middle-class people, who were extremely conventional, and there had been considerable discord in the family because they strongly disagreed with his way of life and his mode of dress. As a result of this, he moved out of their flat in Putney, and went to live with his married sister who lived

40

nearby.

The case was adjourned for report, and before he left the Court, I saw him in my office, and made an appointment to see him there the following Thursday morning. I also telephoned his parents and arranged to call and see them. On the morning he telephoned me and said that he could not keep the appointment because his sister's baby was ill and he was looking after it. His sister had a part-time job, but he was unemployed and had agreed to stay in, to be at home when the doctor arrived. He sounded quite anxious about the baby, so I told him that I would come to his sister's house and interview him there.

Later that morning, I arrived at the house, and he opened the door, looking fairly worried.

'Come in, Mr Mott, I thought you might be the doctor.'

'He hasn't been yet then?'

'No.'

'In that case, I'd just like to ask you one question.'

'Yes?'

'If, when the doctor arrives, he looks like you – are you going to let him examine the baby?'

Later I visited his parents who told me that he was a really nice lad, but he had become a hippy and now nobody wanted to give him a job. He had very little money, but a few months ago they gave him a record player for his birthday because he loved music.

'You did what?!'

We gave him a record player.'

'Let me get this straight – you came home one day and found that your kitchen door window had been broken, and you called the police?'

'Yes.'

'And the only thing that had been stolen was your son's record player?'

'Yes.'

'And he subsequently admitted he had done it – and the police charged him?'

'Yes.'

'With stealing his own record player.'

'Oh.'

'Would you have minded him coming into the flat?'

41

'Of course not, but we didn't know it was him at the time.'

'Didn't the police tell you that they were going to charge him?'

'Not at the time, no.'

'Did you tell them that it was his own record player?'

'Well no – nobody asked us who it belonged to.'

On the day that he reappeared in Court, the police officer in the case did not attend. I was obliged therefore to tell the Court police inspector the whole story. (Have you ever seen a police inspector have a fit?)

I had no choice but to explain to the magistrate that, prior to presenting reports, there were certain facts that should first be reported to the court because it seemed that the accused was charged with stealing his own record player . . . !

The case was adjourned until two pm for the police officer, and the lad's mother to attend.

A veil shall be drawn over the afternoon's proceedings, but the magistrate agreed to a change of plea and then the case was withdrawn. I often wonder what might have happened if the Court had not requested a social inquiry report.

☆   ☆   ☆

We, in the service, all make mistakes, so just to show that I am human too . . .

It used to be the practice to provide pre-trial reports in cases that had either been committed for, or elected, trial at a higher court. I was asked to prepare such reports for the Kingston Crown Court on a man who had defrauded the well-known company for whom he worked as a computer operator.

What I didn't know at the time was that I was dealing with a very slippery customer indeed. It was a large company and they paid their employees by cheque, which was issued by the computer and paid directly into the employee's bank account. In some mysterious way, the name of a fictitious employee had become inserted into the list of staff, and for several months a fairly substantial cheque had been paid into an equally fictitious bank account. Guess who was drawing the money!

There are usually quite a few weeks before committal and the actual hearing, but in spite of repeated requests, he failed to attend my office for interview. Eventually I was notified that the case was coming up on the following Monday for trial, and reports were required urgently. After dire threats etc., he eventually kept an appointment with me on the Friday morning prior to the trial. I now realized that he was indeed a very difficult man to interview.

I have already stated that reports should be reliable and accurate both in the interests of the client and the court. He told me that he had two other private businesses and although he made some money on one of them, he lost on the other, so that there was very little income except for his salary as a computer operator, and he had now lost that job. He agreed that he had taken several thousand pounds from his employer and said that he had been advised to plead guilty when he appeared in Court next Monday. He wanted a chance to repay the money, and as a show of good faith he had, upon the advice of his solicitor, paid £1,000 into Court already. It all sounded fairly authentic, particularly if he was to plead guilty, and I felt sure that he would do so because he had admitted both the offence and how he had carried it out to me in the office.

Owing to the shortness of time, I rushed the report through – against my better judgement – outlining the background exactly as he described it. I managed to get it typed and sent off in time to arrive for Monday's hearing.

The following Monday I was sitting in my office at about midday, when the telephone rang. It was the Senior Probation Officer at Kingston Crown Court.

'Mr Mott?'

'Yes.'

'I have a message for you from His Honour Judge John Ellison, of Kingston Crown Court.'

'Yes.'

'Have you got the £1,000 because we haven't got it!'

The accused had pleaded guilty, and had now been remanded into Wandsworth Prison for three weeks for me to prepare up-to-date reports.

Oh brother!

For the next three weeks this case had top priority.

Yes, he had two businesses – one was fictitious in an empty shop with books showing trade deficit. He was an undischarged bankrupt. I discovered two cars hidden away which interested the Official Receiver etc., etc.

43

I eventually attended court in person where I presented a fully comprehensive and accurate report, much to the amusement of all in Court.

But not, I'm afraid, the accused.

Happily, embarrassing situations such as this are few and far between. The preparation of reports to the Court are often quite straightforward and the defendant is usually glad of the opportunity to discuss the problems related to the commission of the offence. The probation officer will make a recommendation to the Bench and it will be considered together with other relevant information, prior to sentence. Having asked for a report, the Bench usually evaluate the information contained there, and often act upon it.

On some occasions, certain information may, in the long run, do more harm than good, and I well remember preparing reports on a young man who had been told by the magistrate that he would be committed to a Detention Centre. Reports, at that time, were in accordance with Home Office directions, prior to a Detention Centre committal. During the remand period I discovered that this young man had homosexual tendencies and, considering his personality, I felt him to be unsuitable for a Detention Centre. Now, if I included my reasons for thinking this in my report, his solicitor was entitled to a copy of that report, and it would therefore be seen by his parents, who had accompanied him to Court on previous appearances. I decided to consult the magistrate before the Court sat, because in some courts, reports were read in advance to save Court time. This case was one of them.

'May I mention the case of . . . ?'

'Ha,' he said. 'That's the lad I'm going to send to Detention Centre this morning!'

My report was lying on his desk and he obviously hadn't read it. I looked at him. 'I beg to differ, Your Worship, but that's the lad you're going to put on probation this morning.'

He looked at me and smiled. He sat back in his chair – threw up his hands and said: 'I'm open to argument!'

'Perhaps if you read the report, sir?'

He took the point.

☆ ☆ ☆

One time, I went to the Alton Estate at Roehampton to visit a

44

lad and his parents as part of the preparation of a Court report.

It is a vast estate of many high-rise flats, and I was the Probation Officer assigned to that area. When the estate first opened there were quite a number of offences committed, relating to the taking and driving away of motor vehicles and motorcycles. These were often found abandoned on a Sunday morning, and it emerged that some of the youngsters, newly settled on the estate, were returning to their old haunts on Saturday night, and borrowing other people's transport in the early hours of Sunday morning, to get back to Roehampton.

When the police realized what was going on, a special patrol put a stop to it fairly soon. On this occasion, the family I was visiting had lived there for about four months, and should, by now, have settled in reasonably well.

Unbeknown to me, I had been given the wrong address, although the actual block was correct. I rang the bell and a lady answered the door. 'Good morning, are you Mrs . . . ?'

'She's gorn.'

'Gone?'

'Yes, gorn to Holland, left her husband and them two poor little buggers, to look after themselves. She's gone to live with this bloke she met on holiday – he's Dutch and he's got a pub or something – yes, she's been gorn about six weeks.'

'I've got the wrong flat then?'

'Oh – yes – three doors down luv, just up there.'

'Thank you very much.'

She didn't even ask me who I was or what I wanted. I went to the correct flat and a gentleman opened the door.

'Are you Mr . . . ?'

'You must be Mr Mott, please come in.'

'Is your wife at home?'

'You've just missed her. She's gone down to Putney, shopping.' And to the lad whom I had come to see, who was also present . . . 'Hasn't she, Tom?'

Tom nodded.

'I see . . . oh well, perhaps we will have a talk about Tom's Court appearance. I need to present a picture of the family in general, and Tom, in particular, to assist the magistrates in coming to a decision – anything you may feel to be relevant.'

We went on talking. Then: 'Do you mind if I see Tom's bedroom?'

(Bedrooms tell you an awful lot.)

'No, certainly.'

I moved quickly, up the stairs and into what I knew was the bathroom.

'Oh, I'm sorry, I'm in the wrong room.'

No cosmetics, only three toothbrushes (Tom and his father and brother), nothing feminine at all. By now I was fairly sure that the garrulous neighbour did know something. It was a sad situation, but I had to know.

'Mr . . . I do have reason to believe that your wife may be in Holland.'

The poor man almost broke down. 'How on earth do you know that – we haven't told anybody.'

He was looking at me with what seemed to be a mixture of horror and admiration.

'Would you like to tell me about it?'

He was in tears now – she had left, but they all lived in hope that she might return. Of course it was relevant to the boys' behaviour – especially Tom – he missed her most.

'But how on earth did you know?'

'Well, we find these things out, you know.'

I never told him I went to the wrong address!

Some years later in Sutton I met Frankie, who was a West End prostitute. She was slim and attractive, but in the West End of London she was just another one of 'the girls' and would have been hardly noticeable – however in Sutton High Street she was the centre of attraction.

In spite of her outward appearance, Frankie was emotionally deprived, unloved and desperately unhappy, so it was not really surprising when she walked into a local store and stole – a teddy bear. Of course, she had been spotted, and when the police arrived she was walking slowly up Sutton High Street, clutching this token of affection to her bosom.

She appeared at Sutton Magistrates Court where I was working at the time, and pleaded guilty. She was remanded on bail for three weeks for a report from my colleague in Paddington. This was the area where Frankie lived, and I was obliged to send a request for a report, backed by as much information as was available at the time.

She attracted so much attention from the local lads, not to mention the odd glance from young PCs, that I decided to take her to my office which was less public, in order to interview her. She was very upset and emotional and grateful to get away from the public gaze.

Three weeks later she returned to Court, and having made contact with my female colleague in Paddington, she was much more cheerful. But her appearance had not changed and once again she was the centre of attention in the Court precincts. Once again, I took her to my office and gave her a cup of tea. She had been dealt with by the Court and would now be given advice and guidance by my female colleague. I drove her to the station and put her on a train.

I never did find out why she came to Sutton, but a week later I received a letter from her thanking me for being so kind to her. She has a nice new room in Paddington and would I please come up to tea one afternoon so that she could thank me properly . . . 'Oh, and by the way I am not allowed to have men in my new room so when you come, will you please say you are my Uncle Charlie!'

I wrote to Frankie thanking her for her invitation. I told her that I didn't go to London very often, but if I did I would certainly look her up. I've still got her letter.

☆ ☆ ☆

I went up to Great Marlborough Street Magistrates Court for a case, where I was received cordially by my old friend and colleague, Charles Morgan. The waiting room and foyer were crowded with most attractive young ladies – all West End prostitutes waiting to appear.

As I was surveying these ladies Charles Morgan grinned at me and said: 'You know what their latest gimmick is, don't you?'

'No.'

'They wear mink drawers!'

We went into his office and he called to one of the girls.

'Yvonne,' he beckoned her over and she came into the office. 'Show Mr Mott your drawers.'

Yvonne obliged without hesitation – but I often wonder how Charlie Morgan knew about that.

☆ ☆ ☆

47

In the bigger cities probation officers are often assigned to a particular area, and they often become quite familiar with the surroundings, schools, youth clubs, employers, local hospitals, etc. These are very valuable contacts when approaching outside agencies for help with a case. I always found local people very helpful and there are quite a number of voluntary workers assisting the probation service in differing ways. They usually receive some basic training, and work under the jurisdiction of a probation officer. I recall, however, an occasion when the system of covering a particular area once backfired with almost disastrous results.

Two plain-clothes officers were on duty in Putney High Street when they observed a young man acting suspiciously. They thought that he was loitering with intent to steal from ladies' shopping baskets. It was near a bus queue and he seemed to be hanging about, looking into the shopping baskets. After observing this, the two police officers eventually arrested him and took him to Putney police station. He seemed to be rather illiterate and of limited intelligence. He was unable to give a satisfactory account of himself and he was eventually charged and kept in a police cell overnight. The next day was a Saturday and there was only one duty probation officer available to the Court. The lad gave an address where he said he lived, the police said that there was no such road. The duty probation officer had no local knowledge of the Putney area, and after pleading guilty, the lad was remanded in custody to Ashford Remand Centre, for a period of twenty-one days.

When I heard about this on Monday morning, I was horrified. The young man had said that he lived in Uttrell Avenue, Putney, and I immediately recognized this as being Luttrell Avenue. I was really quite surprised that the police had not cottoned on to the real name, particularly as it is a highly desirable residential area with very nice houses, well-known in the area. I decided that the lad's family really must be notified of his whereabouts, particularly as he seemed a bit backward, and no doubt they would be worrying about him. Luckily I went that same morning to Luttrell Avenue. Then the balloon really went up!

It was a large house, beautifully furnished, with plenty of evidence of university background, rowing caps and even oars decorating the hall walls. I was received by a charming, middle-aged lady who turned out to be his grandmother. She was appalled!

'His father will be absolutely furious; he is in America at present because he is a member of the British Embassy in the USA. He is living in Boston at present. I will send him a cable straightaway about all this. How dare they arrest my grandson.'

I explained how it had all happened, and said that it seemed most unfortunate, but neither the police nor the magistrates had had much choice. She said she would contact his father through diplomatic channels as soon as possible.

I decided to go to Ashford Remand Centre as soon as possible, and the next day I went there and interviewed the lad.

In view of possible further complications, I conducted this interview as thoroughly as possible, but I found him most difficult to interview because of his limited intelligence. He certainly denied any attempt to steal and said he pleaded guilty because he thought it the best thing to do, and because he didn't want his father to find out.

It seems that, in the past, he had not settled in a job, partly because he had no qualifications. His father decided that he should go to sea, to broaden his experience of life. He had duly signed on as a merchant seaman, and had completed a voyage on the day prior to his arrest. An older seaman, trying to be helpful brought him to Wimbledon, and he told me that this seaman left him the next morning, after they had both slept in a railway carriage.

The next day (Friday) he had found his way to Putney, but could not find 'Uttrell Avenue'. He said he was actually asking people in the bus queue about it, when he was arrested.

I told him that I had notified his grandmother who would, no doubt, be visiting him. (In fact, only the family solicitor actually went to see him at Ashford.) During the next two weeks my telephone hardly stopped ringing. Solicitors and even a barrister phoned me for further information. The local police superintendent phoned to tell me that an official complaint had been received about the two police officers in the case: 'Would I give evidence on their behalf if required to do so?'

I said I would.

I decided to give an interim report to the magistrate, in other words, to put him in the picture so that he knew what was going on. There was nothing he could do at this stage, but he looked quite thoughtful.

The family solicitor telephoned – had I written my report yet? I said I had.

'What had I recommended to the Court?'

I said that the actual offence was quite trivial and that under the circumstances the court might consider a conditional discharge. I was surprised when the solicitor said: 'Certainly not. We are going to demand a change of plea, and want the case dismissed – our client is not going to have a conviction against him.'

I suggested: 'If the magistrate agrees to a change of plea, why not, under all the circumstances, ask the police to withdraw the charge?'

'That's a good idea. We've booked him on a flight to Boston in the afternoon, and he's going to join his father!'

I thought this was jumping the gun a bit, but on the given day an army of legal representatives arrived. I was not required to present my report but I was asked to verify information from the witness box. The police withdrew the charge and the bewildered young man was whisked off, presumably to the United States.

I duly provided a written statement on behalf of the two unfortunate police officers, who had, in fact, treated the lad very well indeed. Both officers were completely cleared of any misconduct – and rightly so.

Some weeks later I received a telephone call from the Principal Probation Officer, Mr S. Farmer.

'Mr Mott, we have received a letter from the Commissioner of Police, commending you for your inquiries in a recent case. Congratulations!'

☆ ☆ ☆

Hundreds of reports are produced each week by probation officers for courts, particularly in England and Wales. Not all of them present the problems or upheaval of those that I have described. Sometimes they are fairly straightforward and easy to produce. They are, however, often time consuming, particu-

50

larly when the client is in custody. Quite often they afford the opportunity for a probation officer to meet a prospective client for the first time, and these interviews with subsequent possible recommendations, constitute a very responsible part of the probation officer's job. Certainly they are not to be taken lightly by the officer, the client, and, most of all, the Court.

During these pre-sentence interviews, I only ever met one man that could justify his participation in crime, at least, to himself. He was a blind man who had opened an office as an estate agent. He received certain deposits of cash on various properties, and then converted the money to his own use.

He was subsequently charged, and appeared at Wimbledon Magistrates Court. At that time I was the duty officer there, helping out on a temporary basis. I was surprised that he arrived completely on his own, and he seemed to be very self-sufficient. He did, however, have some difficulty in entering the dock and I went forward and gave him a helping hand. He was committed to a higher court for trial, and released on bail. I helped him from the dock, and he told me that he had a hired car picking him up a bit later. I asked him to come into my office where he could wait, in comparative comfort, until his car came.

I explained that I was a probation officer and asked him if there was anything I could do to help him. He replied: 'I am a blind man; I have just been living a high life on other people's money, night clubs, dinners, women, wine – you name it, I've done it! If you have enough money you can get anything you want in London. I was arrested, taken to the police station, questioned, and then brought to court this morning. Now I am going to the Old Bailey. I will listen to the case – hear the legal arguments all about myself, and then hear the judge pro-nounce me guilty. I will go to prison! I will hear the shouting of the guards, the banging of the doors and the noises made by other prisoners. I will get a warm bunk, three square meals a day, and there will always be a hand to guide me. I will tell my story to others, and listen to the tales they will tell me. What can you offer instead of that? Put me in a home? Thank you, Mr Probation Officer – thanks – but no thanks.'

☆　☆　☆

I remember sitting in my office one morning, prior to the court

51

sitting. A young lady came in, looking a little worried.

'Somebody suggested that I ought to ask your advice.'

'Yes – please sit down – what can I do for you?'

'I'm appearing in court this morning because I forged my mother's name and cashed her cheque – she knew all about it but . . .'

She looked distressed . . .

'Tell me what happened.'

Before continuing with this story I feel I must explain what used to happen at about seven thirty am on Clapham Junction Station. If you went there at that time you would have encountered a small army of ladies known as Mrs Mops. This faithful band of women – most fairly elderly – would be setting forth to do their daily office or shop cleaning in the West End. They were a loyal and trusted band, and most of them had the keys to the various business premises to let themselves in. There was an unwritten rule amongst them that they did not let their employer down, so that, if for some reason they were unable to get there, they often found a substitute such as a relative or neighbour, to go in their stead. The employers, for their part, were usually well aware that this was taking place but as long as the cleaning was done, didn't mind. They would, however, make out a cheque to the 'official' cleaning lady if not paying cash, and this could sometimes complicate matters.

No doubt you will by now have realized the story told to me by my young lady visitor. Yes – she had taken her mother's place and had attempted, with mum's consent, to cash her cheque. A most serious offence, according to the law! When she appeared in court later that morning the magistrates were at first inclined to take a serious view of the situation.

'Do you wish to say anything about this offence?'

'I would like the probation officer to speak for me please.'

'Do you know her, Mr Mott?'

'Sir, this young lady was seriously injured in a road accident about eighteen months ago. She has desperately tried to find work since, but has been unsuccessful, partly due to the fact that she has only one leg.

'She can't even get a job as an officer cleaner, so she takes on work at times for her mother to try to earn a few pounds, which they share. Mother was sick at the time and this young lady signed her mother's name for the cheque.'

52

The Bench can be surprisingly sympathetic at times.

'You will be Conditionally Discharged for twelve months, and Mr Mott will find you a job!'

Thank you, Your Worship.

Sadly, with the development of office cleaning businesses, this loyal band of ladies have become redundant, except on a local basis.

Reg came into my office one day, looking very fed up.

'What's wrong, Reg?'

'I haven't got any work this week, so I won't have cash to give the wife on Friday.'

He always worked for himself, doing decorating, car repairs, etc.

'Look, Reg, I'm going to paint my mother's house soon. If you would like to go and do some preparation for me, I'll give you £25.'

'What will I 'ave to do for £25?'

'£25 worth of work. You decide.'

'OK.'

He went to my mother's house at Epsom and started cleaning down the paintwork outside the house. My parents came out and told him that they were going down the road, shopping.

'Will you answer the phone if it rings, Reg? Say we'll be back in about half an hour.'

'Ain't you gonna lock the door?'

'No, of course not, Reg. Why should we want to do that?'

Later, when they returned, my father 'put his foot in it' properly. He asked: 'My son's a good probation officer isn't he, Reg?'

'No better than any other.'

Dad got annoyed – he stamped inside and closed the door. About an hour later Reg tapped at the door and said to my mother: 'I'm going now, missus.'

'Oh, thank you Reg, thank you for coming.'

He closed the door. Two minutes later the door opened and his head popped round. He looked at my father and said: ''E listens to yer!'

6

SUPERVISION

The supervision of persons placed on probation can be something of a challenge at times, but usually interesting, and sometimes quite exciting. Certainly, there's hardly a dull moment.

The thought is father to the deed, so it is said, and part of the officer's job is to try and influence the client's thoughts about their way of life and anti-social activities. Sometimes this is not too difficult, particularly if there are practical problems which, with a little help and understanding, may be resolved without taking short-cuts. Two heads are sometimes better than one, and the response from clients is often quite surprising. Naturally, the co-operation and goodwill is all-important because genuine reform must come of the client's own volition, and not because of the 'iron fist in the velvet glove', that I referred to earlier.

Yes, there will be failures and there will be times when disciplinary measures must be introduced. The Probation Officer is in place of an alternative sentence, and the original offence is not finally dealt with until the probation order is completed. In the case of clients failing to comply with the conditions of the order, they can be returned to court and dealt with in some other way. Happily, this does not happen very often. Sometimes the response is not very good and it is disappointing when clients let themselves down, and as a result the officer may feel let down too.

We are dealing with different types of characters, different backgrounds, different attitudes and different ways of life, and each case in its turn will probably require a different approach by the officer after due consideration. The types of offences committed also vary considerably, and it is certainly no easy task to supervise thirty or forty offenders with different needs.

After I had been in the Service for about six years I was selected to attend a two-years' course at the Portman Clinic, New Bond Street. This was a course arranged to enable to group of eight probation officers to study a little deeper casework and diagnosis, particularly in cases where there were personality defects, and/or character disorders. These were borderline cases who were not actually suffering from mental illness, but had come before the courts because of irrational behaviour which might be eliminated by greater understanding and counselling. The course was under the jurisdiction of psychiatrist Dr A. Limentani, assisted by Mrs Brabrook, who was an excellent psychiatric social worker.

We met in a group on alternate Friday mornings, when we presented difficult cases for diagnosis. I found this course extremely helpful, particularly in subsequent years, with cases that I may otherwise have had considerably less success with. I would like to mention some of those cases, commencing with one that I took to the Portman Clinic, because I was completely baffled . . .

☆　　☆　　☆

A police car was patrolling at one o'clock in the morning, in Wandsworth, when the officers saw a schoolboy in uniform, riding a bicycle without lights. When he saw them he attempted to take evasive action, and his behaviour aroused a good deal of suspicion. He was stopped and questioned, and could not give a reasonable account of himself or his actions. He was taken to the police station, and he was found to be wearing ladies underwear underneath his school uniform. He lived locally, so the family were notified that he was at the police station, and was about to be charged with breaking and entering and theft. In fact, he had been working as a Saturday boy at a local launderette, and he told his mother that he wanted to experiment in the cleaning of ladies underwear. He persuaded his mother to lend him her underwear for this purpose, and he took it to the launderette where he worked. That night, he had returned to the launderette and broke in. He put on his mother's underwear and was riding home when the police stopped him. He appeared at the local juvenile court and the case was adjourned for reports from myself.

I was already extremely puzzled by his behaviour: I had seen him briefly at my office and he seemed to be a nice quiet, respectable lad. This was later confirmed by his school report. I called at his home where I saw his sister, his uncle, and his mother. His father could not be present because he was working away, but all three of them told me what a nice lad he was. I could not overlook the sexual overtones of the incident, but it did appear to be an isolated instance, and there appeared to be no previous example of possible transvestism.

Well, there's a first time for everything, so, with no greater understanding of the offence than before, I suggested to the court that he should be placed under supervision, primarily for me to keep an eye on him, and possibly help him. One thing was certain: Most youngsters do not behave in such an unusual manner unless prompted by a fairly strong urge to do so. First, I must try and discover the root of the problem. During the next nine months I saw him almost every week and I had no reason to alter my first impression of him. I saw both parents several times and they were both as puzzled as I was. They were inclined to want to forget about the whole incident and write it off as a boyish prank.

It worried me because I felt that there was more in it than that. As I got to know him better, we had some frank talks about sex and adolescent development, but I had to admit – I hadn't got a clue. The fact of getting caught and the subsequent court appearance may have proved a sufficient deterrent, and have brought him to his senses.

I decided to take the case up to the Portman Clinic for analysis. There were eight probation officers in the group, with the Psychiatric Social Worker and Dr Limentani. I gave each of them a typewritten history of the case, and also, verbally, outlined my own feelings about it.

There followed dead silence.

Dr Limentani said 'Well done, you've got it all recorded well.' And that was all!

The group was getting angry because he shot down any suggestions we made. He said: 'You're all getting angry with me because I won't give you a free lecture on transvestism. Mr Mott, take your file back to your office and read it from start to finish, then come back next time and tell the group why he did

56

it!'

(I can recommend that advice, particularly in the light of what followed.)

I took the file back to my office, settled in a chair and read it from cover to cover ... Of course, why the hell hadn't I seen it before!

The next time I saw him I said casually: 'Oh, by the way, how's your uncle? You know, the one I saw when I first met your mother.'

'Oh – him.'

I waited ... 'He wasn't really my uncle, he was mum's friend. Dad was away working when he used to call.' ... He brightened visibly. 'He hasn't been around since I appeared in court.'

No wonder I couldn't find anything in the case – there was nothing to find. He had succeeded in what he had set out to do. It was loyalty to both parents. He didn't want to tell his father about the situation because of loyalty to his mother, but he desperately wanted it to stop. He was so disturbed about it that he wanted to be her so that he could stop it, but he couldn't get inside her – the nearest that the could get to that, was to get into her underwear.

Imagine the extent of his anxiety to have behaved in the way he did. When 'uncle' disappeared from the scene, everything went back to normal. He told me later: 'I'm glad you found out, but I couldn't have told you.'

I told him: 'Now we forget the whole thing, except that you really didn't need to resort to breaking the law.'

Irrational thoughts sometimes lead to irrational actions. He was never in trouble again.

On another occasion, I found a probation order in my tray that had been placed there by the senior probation officer, for me to take up. The man had been made subject of a probation order for a period of one year, for a minor assault. He had one previous conviction for a similar assault about two years before, when he had been fined. The address was that of a local pub – just a small pub in a side street nearby. I wrote a letter inviting him to call at my office and see me, and I took it with me to the pub at lunch-time. I had a beer and a sandwich, and eventually asked the one barman: 'Do you happen to know Colin?'

'That's me.'

I made sure that he was the right person and then quietly gave him the letter I had with me.

'Put that in your pocket – it's private – read it when you've got a moment.'

I should have known better. He opened it there and then.

'Oh, it's OK, they all know about it here. I was driving my car and I got into an argument, and this bloke started to take the piss because of my eyes.'

Colin was completely cross-eyed.

'OK, well, let's talk about it when you come up to the office – this is not the time or place.'

I felt glad though that I had made contact with him because in the absence of reports I had no background information.

Thankfully, courts do not often make a probation order without first having further information. No doubt the court felt that his behaviour on both occasions related to his being cross-eyed. He was quite intelligent and presentable, but had never really had a girlfriend, probably because of his eyes.

After a few months I got to know him quite well, and we talked about many things, but if I attempted to try and discuss eyesight he usually backed off. I came to the conclusion, however, that if he could do something about his eyes, his whole way of life might change for the better. I decided that I shouldn't duck the issue; after all, it was related to the offence for which he was packed on probation.

One day I took the bull by the horns.

'Tell me straight, Colin – we know each other well enough now – could anything be done to straighten out your eyes?'

He looked at me for a long time then said: 'A doctor told my mother once that when I was older I could have an operation that might cure my eyes. She's dead now, and I never went back.'

'Don't you think you owe it to her to follow it up?'

'No, I *** don't.'

He got up and walked out of the office.

He failed to keep our next two appointments, so after about three weeks I dropped in to the pub at lunchtime.

'Where's Colin?'

'Colin has left – don't know where he's gone.'

'Oh.'

I felt responsible for him leaving, and I was fairly certain that he was running away from me because I wouldn't sweep his problem under the carpet. Perhaps I had been wrong, but if I have a maxim, which I strongly believe in, it is to do what I believe to be right, and I still felt that I would have been wrong not to try and discuss it with him.

After six weeks I went to the magistrate to discuss the situation and he suggested that I take no further action on the breach of probation order. I left it on the file and nothing happened for the next few weeks. Then, some three months after he had walked out on me, there was a knock on my door.

'Come in.'

He came in – he stood at my desk with a smile on his face, looking at me with the clearest pair of brown eyes!

'Bloody hell, Colin, you've had 'em done.'

'I'm sorry I walked out on you. I nearly punched you in the face. When I cooled down I knew you were right – about my mother I mean – so I went back to the doctor and he fixed it all up. I look in the mirror now and realize what a bloody fool I was. I've come to thank you.'

'Colin, looking into those eyes is the best thank you I'll ever get.'

☆　☆　☆

The experience I gained at the Portman Clinic, not only helped me to a deeper understanding of the problems of clients, but it also changed my own outlook toward their behavioural problems. It is sometimes better to wait and see than rush into things, and in probation work, the old cliche: 'When in doubt, do nowt' can often apply. There is a lot of difference between making a fairly accurate diagnosis, and coming up with an instant cure. The job of the probation officer is to impart to the client a greater understanding of his own behaviour and the possible reasons to which it might be attributed. Any permanent changes for the better should come from the client. It is sometimes easier said than done – but not always . . .

One client was a tall, pale, intelligent young man, and came from a nice local family. His father had died a few years earlier, and mother was now the breadwinner, assisted by him and his sister. He walked into a tailor's shop and purchased a pair of trousers, which he paid for by cheque. The shop assistant immediately noticed that there was a female name on the cheque and the signature was an obvious forgery. The police were called and he was arrested and charged. The chequebook belonged to his sister.

I interviewed him alone and then together with his sister and mother. They were a very close-knit family, and all were worried about the situation. He could not account for his actions and mother said that he had only to ask and she would have paid for the trousers. His sister said that she would have signed the cheque if she had been asked – so why did he do it?

After his father died, he decided that he would like to join the RAF. He was an extremely accomplished saxophone player, and he felt that he could get into an RAF band and combine his love of music with a career. Mother told me that both he and his sister were adopted, and both of them knew about this, so that a life in the forces would also make him slightly more independent. Mother was in favour of it because he had taken to playing in 'groups' and at various clubs, and she had a horror of him getting involved with drugs, etc. He had considered this highly amusing and told me that, as a musician, he was pleased to play in any company because he played for the love of music.

He was placed on probation for twelve months, partly because there seemed to be some questions remaining unanswered, which may have had a bearing upon his behaviour. During the next few weeks he called to see me regularly, and I visited the family home a few times, because it seemed to me that that was where the problems might lie.

He told me that he had joined the RAF but he just could not take to the life of a serviceman. He hated every moment of it, and after six months he exercised the option of buying himself out. To do so, he sold his saxophone. Since that time, he had not been involved with music, because he had no instrument. His mother was not in favour of him getting another saxophone because she was still nervous about drugs on the music scene. Perhaps if his father had been alive the situation might have been different but they all seemed to miss him and mother in particular when it came to this sort of decision.

Sometimes, when dealing with a case of this kind – and if you're lucky – you come across a piece that doesn't fit. Don't ignore it – it can be the clue you're looking for.

He came in to see me one evening and after a while he told me, he had signed on to go to evening classes.

'Oh good, what are you going to study?'

'I'm going to learn German.'

'Oh. Why German?'

'Well, with the British and American forces in West Germany, there are a number of groups and bands touring out there. I might manage to get a tour over there later. Anyway, it's something to do.'

I thought about this for some time and then telephoned his mother for an appointment to visit her. I saw her the next day and over a cup of tea I asked her if she would mind answering a question for me.

'Of course. What is it?'

'Was his real mother German?'

'How on earth did you know that? Did he tell you?'

'No, he hasn't mentioned it.'

'I can tell you what it's all about now.'

She looked worried . . .

'It's all about his love for music – it's about getting him another saxophone, and it's about rejection of you, by him, because you won't buy it for him. In other words, you are not really my mother, so I won't ask you for anything – not even a pair of trousers. My real mother is German – I will learn German and then go to Germany and find her – she will let me have a saxophone.'

It was an upsetting interview but at least that was a clear solution – get him a saxophone. This explanation of his actions due to really deep disturbance because of his love of music, did get through to his mother, but she told me that she would first like to discuss it with her family doctor, in whom she had great faith. I promised to call at the end of the week and she could tell me his opinion.

I called a few days later, and when she saw me she smiled. I said: 'Well, what did your doctor say?'

'Get him a bloody saxophone.'

That was not quite the end of the story. I spent the next few weeks helping the lad to understand how the depths of his feelings had almost caused a family upset and certainly, the explanation of his actions had caused some emotional stress to both his mother and sister. He made it up to them. The last time I saw him he was happily married with two lovely children – and a saxophone.

It is easy to be wise after the event, and sometimes, looking back, one wonders if certain incidents may have been either anticipated and/or avoided. As I have already said, the chance to realize what may be important, and put the correct interpretation upon it, may only come about once or twice. This might have applied to a man whom we shall call John. He was an elderly man, but he looked a lot older than his actual age. He had a wife and two children, and she was comparatively younger both in actual age and appearance.

For several years he had begun to take an interest in religion, to the extent that it had almost become a manic, but without anybody realizing the depth of his feelings. His wife knew that he studied the Bible and often spoke about it at home, but she was inclined to take it lightly and let him get on with it.

And then one evening he told her that he felt that she and the children ought to be sent to a 'better place'. She realized that he was unbalanced, and tried to reason with him, but he held her virtually a prisoner at knife-point in the kitchen until, when she turned her back on him, he stabbed her through the back of her neck. Realizing now that he had done wrong, he left the home and was later arrested. He was obviously a very disturbed man. His wife had been found by a neighbour, who had notified the police, and sent for an ambulance. By some extraordinary miracle she later recovered.

This unfortunate man was suffering from mental illness, and after considering psychiatric reports he was eventually committed to the Netherne Mental Hospital. I had prepared reports for the court, and had been able to assist the family to become re-established in a local flat, once his wife was fully recovered.

I visited him at the hospital on several occasions and it became obvious that he was likely to be in hospital for a very long time. Each time I saw him, he confided in me that the world was going to end on 9 September, and he would produce a sheaf of papers on which he had written various figures in the form of mathematical problems, all, surprisingly enough, finishing up with number nine. I passed all this information on to the nursing staff, but mostly it was known to them already. He really was very deeply disturbed, and I could not do anything other than act as a visitor with occasional news of his family etc., on a purely unofficial basis.

Netherne Hospital was an excellent hospital with extensive grounds and gardens for patients to walk in when the weather permitted. It is bounded on one side by a railway cutting, and has to be approached by a crossing over the railway.

☆ ☆ ☆

On 9 September, John had gone for a walk in the grounds. He tried to cross over the railway on a small bridge carrying a pipeline. He fell to his death under a passing train.

Happily, very few cases have such a tragic ending, and it is most rewarding when the probation officer can feel that success has been due to his own efforts, combined with the co-operation of his client. Successful supervision can be about good relationships and favourable response, beginning sometimes with what looks like a hopeless situation. But success comes from unexpected places, and is all the more encouraging when it comes in this way.

One of the cases that perhaps gave me the most satisfaction, was the case of a man, aged forty-three, who had been indecently exposing himself for nearly thirty years. He had been on probation before, had been to prison and had been in a mental hospital. No form of treatment had yet had any effect upon his behaviour, and no form of punishment had yet acted as a sufficient deterrent. Now, he had done it again, and almost out of despair, the Court placed him on probation for a period of three years.

He had recently moved into my area and although I had not prepared reports, or even seen him before, he was placed under my supervision. I read all the reports and previous documents and I gave it a great deal of thought. After thirty years, what chance had I got?

Well, something had to be done. Let's begin at the beginning . . .

Great oaks from little acorns grow, but we all know that if we dig up the tree and look for the acorn we're never going to find it. The fact remains that it had existed at one time or: no oak tree.

Something, about thirty years ago, had triggered off the first of a long series of indecent exposures which had continued ever since. Why had this started at all? We met for the first time in my office and he told me that he had been married for over twenty years and had a very attractive daughter. Both his wife and daughter knew of his previous convictions and had both stood by him over the years. He had a good job and had no monetary problems.

He could not account for the repeated offences of indecent exposure. He said that it always worried him and particularly his wife because she never knew when the police might be knocking at the door. He said he had tried to stop but could not understand how or why this sudden urge would take over. He would like to be able to stop for good – but how?

This was the first of several interviews in which we tried to trace the initial cause of the problem. He told me that he first exposed himself at the age of fourteen, and we looked at the existing circumstances at that time. It was here I got my first clue.

His mother had died several years earlier and when he was fourteen his father had remarried. She was, he recalled, a very attractive woman and he liked her very much. She was thirteen years older than he was, and his father was thirteen years older than her. He admitted he was sexually attracted to her, but her attitude towards him, he thought, was over-authoritarian, and in fact she kept him in his place. Why do you prefer my father to me, he thought? Am I not just as much a man as he is – look everybody – I am a man. Could this be the situation which had triggered off a lifetime of offences?

When we compared some of the subsequent offences, there did not, at first, seem to be any similarities, particularly with sexual overtones. The acorn had disappeared! We're left with the oak tree – in the form of the stepmother.

Can it be, then, that the sexual overtones had now become secondary to stepmother's dominant personality? The need to stand up to her and be a man, still manifesting itself in exposure? This looked better.

He had been going to work in his car when he saw a workmate whose car had broken down. He stopped but went on to work after agreeing to clock his mate on. He was doing this when he was spotted by the foreman, who gave him a dressing down in front of the other man. Result: indecent exposure.

I thought it was rather like opening a safe. When the correct set of emotions clicked into place – exactly fitting those aroused in him by stepmother – he resorted to the same reaction.

'But you must know you're going to do it – why not take some evasive action, or control it yourself?'

'I never linked it with my stepmother after all these years.'

'Can you see it now? Enough to recognize the symptoms and take evasive action?'

'I'll certainly try.'

'OK. Here's what we'll do. You know enough about the background now to be on your guard if you are worried or upset in a manner that may trigger it off. Get to a telephone as soon as possible and phone me at my office. If I am not here speak to my secretary for as long as you like – all about Chelsea Football Club!'

'Chelsea – why Chelsea?'

'Because you are unlikely to phone and say that you feel like indecently exposing yourself.'

'Oh – right.'

'You go to Chelsea quite a lot with your wife don't you? And I follow football too, so there's nothing to feel self-conscious about. I'm hoping, assuming we've got it right, that it will let down the tension and get your feelings back to normal. Anyway, we've nothing to lose, and it might work.'

For the next eighteen months we carried out this plan, the calls getting fewer and fewer because he began to feel less need to rely upon the call. I was feeling that it was actually beginning to work, when an incident occurred that really seemed to indicate a measure of success. I received a phone call from the local police inspector who told me: 'We've had a complaint about one of your clients, from a bus conductress. She had a row with him on the bus and he started to masturbate a rolled up magazine on the bus.

'Ha, ha,' said the police inspector. 'That's an improvement isn't it?' – But it was!

I was delighted. Eighteen months ago there was no way he could have used a rolled-up magazine. Later, when I saw him in my office he told me that the conductress had had a go at him for pushing and made him feel very upset. 'But I was on

65

the bus Mr Mott, and couldn't get to a phone, so I had to do something else.'

Toward the end of three years' probation I involved his wife in the phone calls, because I wished to ease myself out of the case altogether. We met and discussed it several times but the phone calls became fewer and fewer and he was beginning to come to terms with the emotional side and even cope on his own a lot more.

At the end of the period of three years' probation there had been no actual incidents of indecent exposures, and as far as I am aware there have been none since, that Probation Order was made about ten years ago, and if because of probation supervision his life and that of his family has improved as a result, it does perhaps confirm what I have said – that success comes from unexpected places. Not forgetting, of course, that this type of offence can be very frightening and upsetting for the unfortunate victim.

Every case should be given careful consideration, and although some aspects of the offence look similar, considerable differences can exist in motives and reasons that lie behind the offence.

In an exactly similar type of offence – that of indecent exposure – there was, in one case, a completely different set of circumstances and I relate this as an example because it was relatively simple and far easier to deal with. Human behaviour is like that sometimes but it's not always easier to believe.

They were a very nice young couple – married for just over a year. He had a good job, a nice flat, and they were very much in love. She became pregnant and they were both delighted – it was an ideal marriage situation, and one only had to be in their company to realize. The baby was born and they both loved it. The grandparents rallied round, and everybody was happy.

One day, he stood in a telephone box in Roehampton Lane, and when an attractive young woman sauntered past, he indecently exposed himself. She opened the telephone box and said: 'I am a police officer – you are under arrest.'

And so she was – an off-duty WPC.

He had no previous convictions, and I was quite astounded when, after pleading guilty, he was remanded in custody for full reports. I saw him in the cells and he was in a state of collapse. He had not told his wife about his arrest and she did

66

not know where he was. Now, he would not be going home. Later, I went to his home where I saw his wife; I had the most unpleasant task of explaining the whole matter to her. She was incredulous – she just could not believe it.

'My husband – are you sure you got it right?'

It was very sad.

I took her to Ashford Remand centre and we had a very sensible and rewarding meeting. They were very much in love and nothing was going to alter that. They enjoyed a wonderful sexual relationship based on love and affection. They explained it all to me, and as I have said, it was simple. When he came back to Court there was a rather complex psychiatric report couched in official terms but with no real explanation or recommendation.

I went to see the magistrate prior to the hearing and showed him my report. He read it and then grinned. 'I'm inclined to believe your explanation,' he said. 'They were so much in love that they had sex far too soon after the baby was born. Things had not got back to normal and he thought that in future he would not be big enough for her. He was so worried that he was looking for reassurance – a gasp of admiration from the opposite sex – unfortunately he picked on a policewoman.'

He seemed amused. 'What do you suggest I do with him?'

'Er – conditional discharge?'

'That would seem to be appropriate!'

☆   ☆   ☆

There are cases which, at first glance seem to be fairly straightforward, but which turn out to be quite tragic. When a probation officer becomes involved with a client, there is always the possibility of becoming involved with other members of the family, particularly when the family background relates strongly to the behaviour and lifestyle of the actual client. It is generally agreed that an officer should not become over-involved, but sometimes there are reasons why it is difficult to say no. Other members of the family almost become clients on a voluntary basis. These sort of cases must each be taken on their merits but one such case still stands out in my memory after many years. In relating the cases that I have referred to so far, I am anxious that, on looking back, there is a lesson to be learned. This case taught me that you can't set the world to rights, even though my actual client seemed to come out of it all right.

He was a very bright young man; well-mannered and intelligent. He could be most charming and everybody liked him, a fact which largely contributed to his downfall. He found it quite easy to borrow money or obtain credit – easier in fact than getting a steady job. He lived with his mother and his stepbrother in a luxury flat at Putney, and on the surface they appeared to be well off and living in comfortable surroundings. The whereabouts of his own father were unknown, and the father of his stepbrother was a serving army officer, so mother and the two boys lived happily together, although the youngest boy was aged only six. Nigel was an accomplished artist and also an excellent cricketer so when he charmed his way into Pollington Borstal he became an immediate favourite with the other boys and staff alike. Of course he became cricket captain and to his credit he became the only borstal boy that I ever met that served only the minimum sentence of six months.

He came out on licence, and I was instrumental in getting him a job as an artist and designer with a firm that manufactured stage scenery. Again, to his credit, he was very successful in this job, and went on to further his career as a backroom boy in the world of entertainment. The stage did seem to be set for better things to come. But one Friday morning at about nine thirty am I received an urgent phone call.

'Mother's dead!'

It had come as a terrible shock when he discovered her body that morning, having taken her own life. He was at home now, with his little stepbrother, not knowing which way to turn. I went there immediately and found that the police had been notified and all that could be done was being done. She had left a note indicating that she had been under extreme pressure in recent months and could no longer cope.

The little boy, whom we shall call Ben, was still at home and in a state of bewilderment. It was thought best not to tell him, at this stage, that his mother was dead. The Child Care Officer arrived but with some embarrassment because there was no immediate place for Ben to stay.

It so happened that I had two very good friends, Bill and Brenda Murcer, who were wardens at the Church of England

Children's Home in Balham. I telephoned them and as usual they were most sympathetic and agreed to admit Ben on a temporary basis, until more permanent arrangements could be made through the Children's Department. Later that day I took him there and he was made welcome and comfortable. Nigel would stay at the flat until all the affairs were settled, and these arrangements gave us all some breathing space.

I had now become very much involved in the situation, when my role was really supervising officer for a client on borstal licence. But, as I have already said, it sometimes becomes inevitable that your duty to your client leads you into a wider field of activity. Nigel was obliged to give up the flat, but his job was going well, and in typical fashion he obtained a flat in an equally affluent block in Victoria.

For several weeks I kept in touch with Ben, who had become a firm favourite with the Murcers and seemed to have settled in well. His birthday was on 20 September, and I called in to see him with a present and card, but found him very withdrawn. Brenda told me that he had still not been told that his mother was dead, and he had been hoping to have a present from her. I certainly hadn't realized that nobody had told him, and they all said that they just could not bring themselves to tell him. I decided that this situation could not be allowed to continue.

I sat down with him and we had some tea and I broke the news to him as gently as I could. It came as a relief because he said that he really thought that this might be the case but nobody told him. I suggested that we took the football out on the back field and had a kick about – it might take his mind off things. Some of the other kids joined in, and he did at least enjoy his birthday as much as possible. I arrived home at about nine fifteen pm and at first my wife was not too pleased with me. We were supposed to be having friends round for a meal that evening. You see – 20 September happens to be my birthday, too!

There were eventually some legal problems to sort out and at the end of the day Ben went to a permanent home on the South Coast. It was a nice small and cosy home – clean and homely, but the one snag was that all the beds had horsehair mattresses. The solicitor who handled the legal affairs was my friend Neil Maclean. I phoned him and told him about the horsehair mattresses. Next week in court Neil passed round the hat amongst his legal colleagues and came up with enough money to equip the home with interior sprung mattresses.

Solicitors are not all bad! Er, well, you know what I mean!

☆ ☆ ☆

The cases that I have described so far, all serve to illustrate the type of problems that may confront a probation officer anywhere in the country. I have related the details of actual cases that were known to me, partly to show the type of character that any officer many have to supervise. Sometimes it is not too hard to pinpoint the cause of the trouble, but to get the client to understand and accept it, is often very difficult. Having got that far, the object of the exercise is to help the client to remedy the possible basic cause of unacceptable behaviour – not so easy, but not impossible. Anyway, one can have aims and objectives and do the best one can. It takes two to make a bargain.

There are times when decisions have to be made for and on behalf of both the client and the general public as a whole. Sometimes such decisions are not easy to make and even involve a degree of uncertainty. When this situation arises I would rely on my own maxim – do what you believe to be right. Not everybody always thought the decisions were the correct ones, and on such occasions one sometimes had to stick to one's guns in the face of adversity. I would like to demonstrate this by recalling a case where I found an unexpected ally, who presumably thought the same way as I did.

I was working at Sutton Magistrates Court at the time when I met Mark. He was just seventeen when I first met him. He came from a nice family and was always clean and tidy and presentable. He was also quite nice looking and polite, which was later to contribute to his problems. His mother was extremely ill at the time, and his father was not all that well either, which meant that neither of them were able to give Mark the attention that he needed.

Mark was, to say the least, of low mentality and totally unable to fend for himself in society. While his parents were alive, he was looked after properly, fed and clothed, but alas, both parents died within a short time of each other, and this left Mark homeless.

His parents had occupied a council flat which Mark could not possibly have kept up on his own. He had been put on probation for a minor offence, partly due to his desire to go along with others and not be left out. This was to prove a problem for as long as I knew him. I had psychiatric reports and felt that he might need special treatment at a hospital in Epsom. There was, however, the immediate problem of somewhere to live and I managed to get him a place in a special hostel, because he had attended a special school for low IQ pupils. It was a good hostel, and Mark settled well at first, but he could not accept the fact that he could survive for only a short time if he had no support and guidance. He wanted a job, and as I have said, he was presentable and polite, but he completely lacked powers of concentration or a sense of responsibility. With the best intentions in the world, he would set off for work, but fail to arrive there. I would find him in a local cafe or on a street corner with no feelings of guilt or shame for letting people down.

It was, of course, not his fault. His was an inadequate personality, and he would always, in my opinion, need support.

One practical problem that always arose was lack of money, because although he lived on social security and grants for his lodgings, he would constantly find himself out of benefit because he was deemed to have left his job of his own volition. I had many discussions with the DHSS about him but his general appearance gave no indication of his personality problems, and I found it almost impossible to convince them. When he once again became homeless I had the greatest difficulty in finding yet another place for him. I had further psychiatric reports, and managed to get him into another special hostel where he stayed for a time, but he would disappear for several days and would tell me he had stayed the night with a male friend. I was deeply suspicious about this relationship, but as far as Mark was concerned, it was a means to an end – a bed for the night.

Once again I was obliged to seek accommodation, and I was acutely aware that he was fast becoming a cross I had to bear – how could I let him down when he always came back to me when all else failed.

I got him into a hostel at Richmond and I begged the

warden – PLEASE *don't* get him a job. Three days later the
warden phoned me triumphantly. 'I've got him a job – he's a
road sweeper – he has a handcart and is sweeping the road up
in the High Street.'

It was in the High Street the next day that they found the
handcart abandoned – and no sign of Mark. Several weeks
went by, and then a phone call from the police in London.
Mark had been told, by an older man, to go into a jewellers
shop and bring out a tray of rings. When he did so, the man
snatched the rings and ran, leaving Mark outside the shop
where he was arrested. The man was caught later and the rings
recovered.

After further court appearances, various reports etc., Mark,
now homeless, was sentenced to Borstal Training. Now although this seemed to be tragic at the time, it did serve as a
respite and was in fact just what Mark needed. He went to
Feltham Borstal (now a Youth Custody Centre) and strangely
enough he was happy there. He was living in a structured
society similar to a hospital. He had to keep to the rules, as did
the other lads – and he was one of them. At last, he actually
belonged with others. He worked in the kitchen, washing up
etc., and was never any trouble. I gave it a lot of thought.

It seemed that he needed this sort of environment after his
release, for his own sake, and at the present time there was no
existing plans for his future. One thing was certain, I was not
going to allow him to go back to London on his own. I
telephoned a doctor at a hospital at Epsom. He had seen Mark
on a previous occasion and knew about his background and
personality. He thought that he could find a place for him, but
it would be necessary to interview him prior to his release from
Borstal. I felt that that could be arranged on home leave, so we
made tentative arrangements to do just that. Before I could
make any further arrangements, I received a request to attend
a case conference at Feltham, to be chaired by the resident
psychiatrist. I duly went along and I took with me a young
lady student probation officer.

I was expecting a general discussion about Mark's welfare,
and his future, but I was certainly not expecting the method
adopted by the psychiatrist. There was a ring of chairs around
the room with one chair in the middle of the room for Mark.
Various people were to sit around him in a ring and discuss

him, while he sat in the middle. One of the prison officers in charge of a wing, was present, as was a junior doctor who was also on the borstal staff. I discovered that a probation officer from Inner London was also in attendance, having been invited to attend by the psychiatrist. This lady knew nothing about Mark whatsoever, and indeed it became clear, that none of them knew very much about his background or behaviour outside borstal.

I was appalled at the setting in which I found myself, and particularly upset at the thought of Mark being made the subject of this embarrassing situation. I told the group that there was no way that I would take part in this meeting. I also pointed out that, as Mark's probation officer, I would be making all the arrangements about his after-care and that completely excluded any return to Inner London, which would be sure to have disastrous results. At this point I took my leave, together with a much bewildered probation student.

Do what you believe to be right! Well, I had certainly done that, but now I was on my own with Mark, once again. Or was I? . . .

The next day, still feeling indignant, I received a phone call from the senior prison officer who had been in the group.

'Mr Mott?'

'Yes.'

'I just want you to know that I agree with everything you said yesterday – that boy needs treatment – he is a very nice lad, and if I can help you in any way, please let me know.'

I thanked him very much. I told him that I had been in touch with a doctor at an Epsom Hospital but the doctor wanted to see Mark prior to release.

'OK – look, you fix up the appointment with the doctor, then let me know the time and date and I'll bring Mark to the hospital and then bring him back here.'

'That's terrific.'

I couldn't really believe my ears. The next day I received a letter from the junior doctor at Feltham. It simply said: 'Good luck with Mark – if I can help in any way please let me know.'

The Officer duly brought Mark out of Feltham where he was interviewed by a specialist doctor. He felt that Mark should be admitted to hospital upon his release, provided that he agreed. It was hoped that, with treatment, he might become much more self-sufficient. My officer friend arranged to bring Mark himself to the hospital on the day of release, and this he did. I was more than grateful for his support. He was undoubtedly one of the dedicated officers who regard the job of working with youngsters as a vocation; a dedicated group of men.

At that time, borstal licence was for a period of twelve months, and I kept in touch with Mark for the whole of that time. The hospital welfare officer made arrangements about his discharge after his licence had terminated. I was told that he had matured considerably, and they knew of no other offences involving him. I do know that he went to live with a family in Scotland and I think he's married now.

I supervised that case after I had moved to Sutton in South West London in 1968. The clients and the basis of probation work remains the same, but some offences do relate to 'local colour'.

It was certainly not as busy a court as the South Western in London, and I was a bit startled when, on my first day at Sutton a young man pleaded guilty to wilful damage of a shop window. He was ordered to pay £137 compensation. Now, at that time, the maximum amount of compensation allowable by law was only £100.

I wrote a note to the Clerk of the Court on which I put: 'The maximum amount of compensation allowable by law is £100.'

I received a note back. 'Yes, but he doesn't know that.'

Help! Where am I?

7

PAROLE

My move to Sutton coincided with the implementation of the contents of the 1967 Criminal Justice Act, the most important of these being the legalizing of release on parole licence. The Act contained several other changes in law, not the least of which was the introduction of suspended prison sentences, and majority verdicts by juries. My experiences as a parole officer commenced therefore at Sutton and continued there until I retired in 1983.

But this was a totally different ball game. Prior to 1967 the probation service was concerned primarily with the supervision of those on probation; Borstal and Detention centre licence, and voluntary prison after-care. Probation officers were also very much involved in the juvenile courts and I recall supervising youngsters who had been brought before the court under the Education Act because of truancy.

Prison after-care was largely the responsibility of outside agencies such as the Central After Care Association and other most excellent organizations, some of which are very much alive today and still doing an excellent job. The Prison Welfare Officers worked inside the prisons on a separate service, and did a wonderful job under most difficult conditions. It was essential, under the conditions of the 1967 Act, that many changes took place, and a great deal of preparation was required to bring about these changes in advance, so that the Probation Service was geared to the actual initiation of its new role.

It was not quite as simple as might at first be thought. For instance, there were changes in the Children and Young Persons Act. Approved School After Care was discontinued and the duties in the Juvenile Courts were largely handed over to the Social Services. At that time, the probation service had very little contact with prisons or those subject to prison sentences except on a voluntary basis. But many of the persons serving sentences had been known to a probation officer prior to sentence, and contact was often maintained with that person and their family. The basis for this relationship was however already established because of prior contact. The role of parole officer brought about a change of relationship, particularly in the view of the Home Office, who felt that persons released on licence were actually finishing their prison sentence under the jurisdiction of a parole officer. The type of character that was now to come within that jurisdiction varied considerably. In some cases they were dangerous criminals, but certainly more experienced, more sophisticated, and far more used to responding in a variety of ways, to those in an authoritative position. In other words, many of them knew how to handle us better than we knew how to handle them.

Many of them had already been under the supervision of a probation officer when younger, and were expecting this to be a similar type of experience. There was a great deal of uncertainty on the side of the prospective client and also within the service itself. Nonetheless, as much preparation as possible went into those months prior to the actual date of commencement.

Twenty officers from Inner London, myself included, had been allocated to a penal institution for a period of seven days as part of a residential course. I found myself 'living in' at Redhill Training School, which also had a security wing for possible absconders. It was an interesting experience, partly because the word had got round that I was to report back to the Home Office about the running of the centre. This was not actually true, although I was expected to report back to probation HQ, but it had some very interesting side-effects. Several members of the staff gave me confidential information about what was, or was not, wrong with both the institution and other staff members. I think I was wise enough not to put too much emphasis on this, because it was obviously based on anxiety, and in some cases, insecurity.

We attended various lectures and seminars, and the Institute for the Study and Treatment of Offenders (I.S.T.D.) ran an excellent weekend course which was attended by many different persons involved in the penal or judiciary systems, including MPs, prison officers, judges, probation officers, and police officers. This was enlightening and informative and perhaps ought to be done a lot more often than it is.

We gathered as much background information as was possible in readiness for the effective date. One thing was absolutely certain: whatever the state of readiness of prospective parole officers, there was not a prisoner anywhere in the country, who, on 1 April 1968, did not know their earliest date of parole. There was, of course, a backlog of prisoners who might qualify for release on licence, and they were something of a problem if they resided in the bigger towns. By and large, however, this initial period was handled extremely well by all concerned, not least being the newly formed Parole Board. There were some difficult internal problems as far as supervision was concerned, and senior probation officers were obliged to be very selective when deciding upon the actual supervising officer. One always took into consideration the estimated needs of the client, but now there were other considerations, not least of which was security and sometimes, protection.

Quite often probation officers of either sex are alone in their offices until quite late in the day. There is always the possibility of a dangerous situation developing, and I describe this in more detail later on.

There was now a different type of role to play, with different types of clients and different types of characters. The reformative aim of the probation service was, and still is, the ultimate object when dealing with clients. What would be the result of this now?

I would like to describe some of the cases with which I dealt, and some of the incidents which were in some cases, difficult, sometimes amusing, or even tragic, but certainly most serious when considering that the basic principles may have a lasting effect upon a human being's future existence. This was never to be taken lightly. I remember being asked to take over the parole licence of a rather unruly young man who had hitherto been on probation to one of my female colleagues. He was now serving a prison sentence in Maidstone Prison, and I went there to see him to tell him about the change of probation officer and to discuss his possible forthcoming parole. I had met him several times before and we knew each other quite well

77

even though he had never been my official client.

He was obviously expecting to see his previous probation officer, and when he was brought to the visiting room to see me, he stopped short at the door and said: 'You're not my *** probation officer!'

I looked at him and replied: 'Luckily for you, I think I am!'

☆   ☆   ☆

Quite often I am told, mostly by people who have no actual knowledge or experience of the penal system, that prisons are too soft, or, 'just like holiday camps these days, with television and radios etc.' I do have a stock reply when confronted with this enlightened theory. 'Do you have a television and radio at home? And all home comforts in addition? Well, then, may I suggest that you stop at home for a period of one month and don't go outside your front door. I think you will find that there is more to confinement than free board and lodging, with entertainment provided.'

Prison, of course, does mean different things to different people and there is a great deal of difference between serving a sentence in a category A prison and, at the other end of the scale, in an open prison. So much depends on the other inmates, their characters and personalities.

Perhaps this can be illustrated by two cases which give contrasting views of prison life, in the opinions of the recipients. Not, I may add, without a certain amount of humour.

I have a friend who, prior to his retirement, was a Detective Chief Inspector at Scotland Yard. In view of the content of this story, perhaps he had better remain anonymous, but in any case, I am going back to the days when he was a detective constable at Wandsworth Common police station, and much less experienced. He was in plain clothes, standing outside Hurley's bookshop in Balham High Road, when a disreputable-looking character came up to him.

'Are you a copper, mate?'

'I am a police officer, yes,' replied my friend.

'Well, nick me, willyer?'

'Why? What have you done?'

'I ain't done nothin', but I ain't got nowhere to live, no money, no job, nothin', and Christmas is coming, then there's the winter. What I want is to get six months and that will take me over to next spring. It's bleeding cold sleeping rough in the winter – can't yer nick me for something?'

My friend was a very good-hearted man, and he felt sorry for the old lag, so, perhaps against his better judgement, he said: 'OK. Go into Hurleys and nick a book and when you come out I'll knock you off.'

The old lag duly obliged. He went into Hurley's and after a while he emerged with a book under his coat. My friend walked up to him. 'I am a police officer – can I see what you have under your coat?'

When he saw what the old boy had under his coat, he nearly choked – he produced a copy of *Good Housekeeping*.

'That's no good. Go back and change it for a book on football.'

The old boy duly obliged and back he went – later to emerge with a book under his coat.

'I am a police officer . . .'

He duly appeared at South Western Magistrates Court, and pleaded guilty to stealing a book. After hearing a sad tale, the magistrate asked me to have a word with him and decided to deal with him at the end of the morning.

I saw him in the cells, and he said: 'Tell him I want six months.'

There was very little that I could do about it and I went back into court at the end of the morning.

'Have you seen him, Mr Mott?'

'I have, sir.'

'What do you think?'

'I am afraid, sir, that he will only say that he wants six months.'

The magistrate knew the reason why and he was just as compassionate as the police officer.

'Six months' imprisonment!'

The old boy appeared really grateful.

'Thank you very much, guv.'

☆ ☆ ☆

In contrast, in most cases, when a prisoner is being considered for parole, there is early notification to the Probation Service and the case is, as a rule, delegated to a probation officer, to establish contact. Usually, reports are required about home circumstances and future prospects, if the prisoner is released. There is, therefore, a certain amount of pre-release contact and correspondence both with the prospective parolee and that person's family. Sometimes, however, this contact is not possible and very short notice is given to the Parole Officer prior to release.

John was a typical example of this situation, and when he was actually released on licence, under my supervision, we had never previously met. As is usual in parole cases, I received all the documents relating to him, going back to the trial and sentence, and I always found it absolutely essential to read every word of the case history, in every case. John was an elderly man who had spent most of his life in service in stately homes or the homes of the aristocracy. He was a lonely man, unmarried, and with no intimate contact with the opposite sex. At the time of his arrest he was the butler in such a household, which belonged to a highly respected family. He was well-educated, well-mannered and well-behaved – a typical English butler in the old tradition – 'A gentleman's gentleman'.

When his day's work was done, he would go down to the local village pub and enjoy a drink, and, alas, it was here that he met his eventual downfall. By chance, there were two strangers in the area who were, as it turned out, looking around with the intention of finding a likely home for a break-in. They got talking to John, who had never met this type of character before, and after meeting him on several occasions, they persuaded him to take them home with him. They were, in fact, two men with previous convictions who were spinning him a yarn about their own personalities in order to get invited into the house where he worked. When they succeeded in doing so, to his horror, they stole a variety of valuables and left. Foolishly he tried to cover their tracks because he did not wish it to be revealed that he had in fact colluded with them to some extent. When it all came out, he was extremely upset, but nonetheless he was charged and eventually found guilty. All three of them were sentenced to five years' imprisonment. The family for whom John worked were also extremely upset and did all that they could to help him. Partly as a result of their assistance, he appealed against sentence and it was later reduced to two years' imprisonment by the Court of Criminal Appeal.

Of course, he lost his job and the prospects of finding a similar situation were almost negligible. He applied for parole licence and when all the facts were revealed, he was granted parole after serving only twelve months.

Now John did have a relative living in Sutton, and because of this I was asked to make contact to see if he could be given accommodation until better arrangements might be made. This I did, and I think the Parole Board showed a human touch.

John was due to be released on a Monday, and this was not at all convenient, because his relatives would both be away from home on that day. I telephoned the Parole Board and told them about the case and the arrangements that I was trying to make.

'You couldn't let him out on Friday, could you?'

'Hang on – yes, all right – we'll notify the prison.'

It was as simple as that!

The following Friday there was a knock at my office door and when I said, 'Come in' and in walked the butler. I had never seen him before, but I did not need to ask who he was. He entered the room silently and with head erect, in true butler style.

'Mr Mott?'

'Yes.'

'Good morning, sir, I trust you are well.'

He was really a very nice man, and was never going to be any trouble then, or in the future. After several months he asked me if he could go and live with a gentleman friend in another area, and the arrangements seemed to be suitable, so he moved, and I never saw him again.

But, prior to this, after I had come to know him pretty well, he was sitting in my office one day and I said to him: 'Living as you have done during most of your life, with the best of everything at your disposal, prison life must have been far worse for you than for most prisoners. The food for example – that must have been terrible?'

He looked at me and held his head high . . .

'It wasn't the food, Mr Mott, it was eating it off plastic plates!'

☆ ☆ ☆

If you compare these last two cases with the following one I hope you will get some idea of the institutional differences, and subsequent reactions of prisoners of differing character, each serving a prison sentence, but with a totally different background.

I received prison after-care papers on a young man, then aged twenty-three, who was serving a sentence in Albany Prison. Now this is a top security prison and most of the inmates would not be regarded as suitable for an open prison. A lot of them are rugged characters, serving quite long sentences for serious offences. Part of the penalty of being in a prison such as this lies in the fact that they have to live together in a closed environment, sometimes for a very long time. Life, under these conditions is far from easy, and for some, extremely difficult. This young man had several previous convictions including borstal training, but was still the perpetrator of a quite serious offence.

I had never met him prior to receiving the case papers and my first job was to make contact with him, and eventually visit him. Such a visit is not merely to establish contact, but also to attempt to make some assessment of him, with a view of making some sort of plans for his future rehabilitation. One does not give up hope of bringing about a reformation of character, however bleak the future prospects may seem.

I had visited Albany Prison before, and I was impressed with the visiting arrangements: with small cubicles for interviewing in private, but with prison officers within hailing distance if needed. I thought that this told its own story when compared with the more relaxed visiting arrangements in some other prisons.

When I visited this young man for the first time I could sense that somewhere there was something wrong. He was tall and strong looking; quite wiry and looked physically fit, but I noticed that his hands trembled and his eyes were constantly looking aware. He was, in fact, very much on edge, but since he was with me and under the supervision of the duty prison officer there was no apparent reason for it.

I asked if he was all right and he assured me that he was, but I thought that his eyes filled with tears when we discussed it.

Other than this, it was pretty much a normal interview, with discussions about the future, practical plans about home and job prospects, and his relationship with his parents. He had heard it all before, and so far, there had been no lasting change in his attitude towards committing offences. It was really an exploratory interview, but I left feeling uneasy about him, and I resolved not to leave it too long before I visited him again.

Unfortunately, mainly because of the pressure of work, I did not visit him again for about three months, and at that time he was being considered for release on parole licence. I was obliged to provide a home circumstances report to the Review Committee, and it was this that prompted me, once again, to travel to the Isle of Wight and visit him. I sat in my visiting cubicle and he was escorted to see me. Imagine my horror when I saw a livid scar down the side of his face.

'How on earth did you get that?'

He broke down and burst into tears.

'I can't stand it here Mr Mott. If they, the other prisoners, don't kill me, I will kill myself.'

He would not give me any details of what was happening but he was obviously in a very bad mental state and under a great deal of pressure. I formed the opinion that, if he was not to be released upon licence, he should be removed from Albany Prison because of a definite risk of mental breakdown. Remember, he was only twenty-three years of age.

I went to see Ken McBride, the Senior Welfare Officer, who was most sympathetic, and said he would try to keep an eye on him. But we agreed that I should put my feelings into my report to the Review Committee. This I did – in the strongest possible terms – and although I am quite prepared to admit that there was much more in this situation than I knew about (the whole thing might have been due to his own behaviour) nonetheless, it was my opinion that the prison authorities do have a responsibility for the welfare of those under their jurisdiction. It seems that the authorities also shared that view because I was notified several weeks later that he had now been transferred to Wormwood Scrubs.

He was not granted release on licence, so that, when he was eventually released, he became a voluntary case. He had established an address in Tooting, not far from his parents, but no longer under my jurisdiction.

Nonetheless, he called to see me twice at my office in Sutton, and thanked me for helping him. I don't know if he ever got into trouble again, but I do believe that, when problems such as these arise, we have a duty to do what we believe to be right, in the best interests of justice.

In the three instances that I have quoted, I hope that it has become apparent that there are vast differences in the characters of those persons sent to prison, and also their reactions to serving a prison sentence. As far as the Parole Officer is concerned, the problems of rehabilitation are very much related to the individual, and no two cases can ever be the same. The future attitude of the client is all important, and it is not until that person is released from prison, that the actual effect of serving a prison sentence may be realized.

But let's not get too serious at this stage. I will tell you more about parole, and the supervision of more serious criminals later.

On a lighter note . . .

I telephoned Wandsworth Prison to make an appointment to see an inmate, prior to putting in a home circumstances report. I was asked if I could possibly see him at one thirty pm because this was a convenient time for them. The officers' shift changed over at about that time and being the lunch hour, the interview rooms were usually available. Always being anxious to co-operate, I duly arrived at the prison at one thirty pm and the officer on the gate booked me in. In those days, prior to the Mountbatten Report, I could walk up to the 'Centre' unescorted (the 'Centre' was the middle Admin block, with various offices). The wings of the main prison were all leading off from the centre. It was here that I waited for the next hour with no sign of the prisoner who I had called to see. At two thirty pm I went to the centre office and explained to a young lady there my predicament. She was very helpful and telephoned the gate to ask about my prisoner. She told the Gate Officer that I had been waiting an hour, and I heard her say: 'Oh, you are rude!' I asked her why she had said that, and she told me: 'He said, tell him he might have to wait another bloody hour.'

'Did he,' said I, with a frown. I walked up to a door marked: 'Deputy Governor' and knocked.

'Come in.'

There, sitting behind the desk, was a lovely man whom I

had met on a previous occasion, Lieutenant Colonel Bob Shebeer, the Deputy Governor. He made me welcome and I apologized for having to come and complain, but . . .

He listened sympathetically and then lifted the telephone. 'Send the Chief Officer up to my office straight away please.'

The Chief duly arrived and Bob told him what had happened. 'I would like a report about the lack of courtesy, Chief, but first will you please get the man that Mr Mott has come to see.'

About ten minutes later, an uncomfortable-looking Chief Officer returned. 'I've got the man, sir, but unfortunately there are no interviewing rooms available now.'

Bob gave a snort, twirled his twisted moustache, then jammed his cap firmly upon his head and grabbed his walking stick which was kept under his arm like a baton. 'Come with me!'

I followed him out and sure enough, everything was full.

'Where's the Governor?' snapped Bob at the unhappy Chief. 'He's not in, sir.'

'Right – come with me.' He opened the door of the Governor's office and sure enough it was empty. 'Right, Chief – go and get the man – Mr Mott can use the Governor's office.'

Now the Governor's office is the holiest of holies and most prisoners rarely, if ever, enter this holy precinct. You can imagine what my prisoner thought of me, when he entered the Governor's office to find me sitting in a high winged chair behind a huge roll-top desk. He was plainly over-awed, and was treating me with unaccustomed respect. This intensified considerably when a trustee prisoner knocked at the door, and presented me with a tray of tea and biscuits.

Well, I thought, at least they are trying to make up for their lack of courtesy. I sat back and drank my tea and continued my interview in comfort.

Well, it would have been continued in comfort, had not the door suddenly opened, and there, on the threshold stood The Governor. He was obviously not expecting to see anybody in his office – he stood there and took in the scene, and then said: 'YOU'VE DRUNK MY BLOODY TEA!'

When attempting to estimate what it is that constitutes successful supervision, the criteria are sometimes, in official circles, judged by the success or failure of the supervising officer in dealing with that case. The ultimate objective of any form of supervision is successfully to bring about a change for the good in one's client. It may come in thought or deed, or in any other form, and if the officer has played his part, he may well regard such success as being, at least partly, due to his own support and expertise.

I think this is generally the case, but there are some cases that would eventually prove to be successful without the aid of a parole officer. The official role is of course essential, but the parolee may well make a success of the rest of their life with his own efforts.

There was one unusual case, which I feel that I can call successful, even though I almost created disastrous results in my misguided efforts to be supportive.

The person involved was an extremely clever man. He was a schoolmaster at a Grammar School where he taught languages (he was fluent in at least five, including Russian). He was married to a charming wife and had a lovely family; they were buying their own house, and their life seemed to be a happy one.

Imagine the shock, when he was arrested for offences against boys at the school where he worked. He was immediately suspended, and although he was on bail waiting trail at the Crown Court, the waiting period put both him and his family under considerable pressure. Nonetheless, they remained very close and his wife stood by him loyally. He eventually appeared at the High Court and was found guilty. The evidence was overwhelming and there could be no doubt about his guilt. He was sent to prison for a period of two years.

In this sort of case it is almost inevitable that he would be barred from taking another post as a teacher, or any post that involved contact with young persons. After release, therefore, there are additional problems of employment, particularly the type of post acceptable to a man of his education and intelligence.

He was eventually released upon licence and he was almost a model parolee. Whatever it was in his personality that prompted the type of offences that he had committed I never discovered. But I did not doubt the love and affection that existed between him and his wife and family. Almost – no thanks to me.

When he was in prison, she came to my office to see me, and I asked her how she felt about this terrible situation. She told me that she loved him and would always stand by him. She could not wait for him to return home. She said that it was a total miscarriage of justice. He was innocent and she knew he was innocent. The court was entirely wrong and an innocent man had been sent to prison.

Now, as I have stated, the evidence was overwhelming, and there could be no doubt about his guilt. I began to explain this to her and was saying that he must be guilty, when I looked at her and saw big tears in her eyes. Thankfully, it suddenly dawned on me: of course, she *knew* he was guilty. She was refusing to accept it because, if she did, it was going to break up the family, and there was I trying to convince her of the fact. I don't know how I managed to change horses in midstream, but thankfully I did so.

We went through the charade of both pretending that we thought he was innocent, and we kept it up right until the case closed. We both knew that we were playing a game, but it kept the family together. During the whole twelve months that he was on licence, he never managed to obtain employment. She found a part-time job, and left him with the children with complete trust. His licence terminated and I never saw either of them again, but three months later, he telephoned me.

'Mr Mott, I had to tell you, I've got a job!'

How do you measure success?

☆　☆　☆

Reg called at my office in Sutton one day unexpectedly.

'My son's fifteen now, Mr Mott. You couldn't see him for me could you?'

'Why, what's wrong, Reg?'

'Nothing really – he ain't broken the law or anything like that, but I'm worried about 'im.'

'But why?'

'The little sod's behaving just like I was behaving when I was his age!'

I grinned at him. 'In that case, Reg, I'd better see him!'

☆　☆　☆

Brian appeared at the Central Criminal Court, charged, together with several other defendants, with Conspiracy to Defraud. The Court was told that goods to the value of over £250,000 had never been recovered. The defendants had established a perfectly legitimate import business in London, and for a while they were trading openly with various firms in Europe. But various offices, in other names, were established, in order to furnish the major office with references, claiming to have traded with it as separate businesses. In this way, credit was obtained at these European firms, and then, on a given date, large orders were placed with all the firms, and after the goods had been delivered the offices in England mysteriously closed and disappeared.

Brian was held by the judge to be the prime mover in this conspiracy and was described by His Lordship as an 'Evil Genius'. But they all received prison sentences, some of them having previous criminal records. Brian was sentenced to twelve years' imprisonment. The strange thing about him, as I was to discover later, was that he was in fact quite a good businessman and would almost certainly have made a success of the business he had already established. To put it into his own words: 'I was just plain greedy.'

Brian had a wife and children, and they lived locally in a well-appointed, detached house which he owned. When I first received the case history, I contacted his wife, and she came to my office to see me. She described him as a Jekyll and Hyde – a man with a dual personality – but a good father and family man. But she did agree that there was another side to him which she knew little about and which he was always reluctant to discuss. Some of his friends and acquaintances were of doubtful character, but she said that she never really knew what he did for a living. He would leave home each morning dressed like a 'city gent' complete with briefcase, etc. Now, however, she was really feeling the pinch and having to live on Social Security. They were threatening to cut off the gas because she had not paid the bill, and she was attempting to borrow money to pay it before it came to that. I asked her why she had not considered selling the house and getting a smaller, cheaper one that would have left her some money over, on which to live. She told me that Brian would never agree to that. The following week I went to Wormwood Scrubs where I met him for the first time.

Once again, visiting accommodation was very limited and I was asked to see him in what was not much more than a large store-room full of cleaning materials. They had put two chairs in there and we sat opposite each other in quite close proximity. He was a big fellow and inclined to be overbearing. I could imagine that he would want to be boss in any sort of company, and the judge's description of 'evil genius' came to mind while we were talking. His eyes seemed to me to be expressionless and I remember thinking that here was a man that it would not be wise to upset. Nonetheless, he treated me with respect, and we had a sensible and satisfactory interview. When I had read the file earlier, I discovered that he had previous convictions for assault, and I wondered why he was possibly being considered for parole. He told me, however, that he had been transferred to the Scrubs in order that he could have an operation in the adjacent hospital after a heart attack. He said that in a strange way he was grateful to the prison authorities because he now had a pacemaker – if he had not been in prison at the time of the attack, he might well be dead now.

During this interview I could sense the description given to me by his wife of a dual personality. The forceful side of his character was necessary, for him to emerge as a leader within the prison regime.

For instance, 'I went to school with Charlie Richardson . . .'

But then . . . 'If I am released on parole licence, you'll get no trouble from me – tell me to report to you at midnight and I'll be there – being under you must be better than being in prison.'

I explained, although he already knew, that the final decision did not rest with me, but considering the pacemaker, I thought he might have a chance. But if not, why not let his wife sell the house and get something smaller. At least she and the children would have some money to live on until he came out?

Now I saw a different side to him. 'That *** house is my investment for the future – I'll deal with that when I come out.'

I left, feeling that at least I had made good contact, although no real plans for the future could be discussed until his actual date of release were established.

Persons serving a prison sentence will sometimes read into a discussion intentions which become very real to them, even though what was intended was merely an exploration of future possibilities. A golden rule for the visitor is never to say you will actually do something, and then not do it.

Two days later, I received a letter from him that seemed to confirm what I had thought: Dear Mr Mott, Tell her to sell the House. Yours . . . . P.S. Brian to you.

That's all it said.

When I showed his wife the letter she said that she would prefer to wait and see if he got parole. If he did, he could deal with it himself when he came home.

A few weeks later I received notification that his application had been successful and he would be released having served seven years of a twelve-year sentence. This meant that he would be under my supervision for a period of twelve months. All of his co-defendants had already been released, so the future period of licence gave me considerable food for thought. Even with this somewhat more sophisticated character the object of resettlement coupled with reform should be adhered to even though the future seemed to be unpredictable. However, experience shows that sometimes a tough exterior is a cover for deeper feelings. Now he was returning to reality – to face his children and return to his wife, to earn his living, now with a pacemaker in his heart . . .

Let's wait and see.

I used to make a rule, that where a man had a wife and family, I would not see him on his day of release, but always gave him instructions to go straight home to them and settle in – in private.

He would report to me at my office the next day, when we would have an official discussion involving his responsibilities, the possibility of recall to prison if he failed to keep to the terms and conditions of his licence – one of which, was not to associate with known criminals. Now it was my turn to show a tough exterior and leave clients in no doubt that whatever their reaction to the rules, I had a duty to the Parole Board which would be totally adhered to.

It is best to get things straight right from the start, then we both know what to expect. I made no exception with Brian, and told him to go straight home, which he was very pleased to do. But at lunchtime he telephoned me.

'Look, I'm not trying to manipulate you but my wife and I wondered if you would like to call in, just for a cup of tea, this afternoon?'

I thought about it. It was his first day home . . . better to agree than refuse, under the circumstances.

'Yes, thank you very much. I'll see you later.'

I called at the house later and saw Brian and his wife. The atmosphere was friendly and they both seemed to have something to tell me. Eventually he told me that he never thought that he would ever speak to a probation officer in this way, but his wife had told him that I had given her support whilst he was inside and now he realized that everything depended on our future relationship. He seemed, in a way, to be grateful for the chance. On looking back I wonder if he realized that his health was giving him more concern than anybody else had realized. He produced a bottle of brandy. 'Shall we have a drink to the future?' Well, why not?

His daughter came in and said hello. While she was there she referred to Uncle Alan . . . I knew she was referring to one of his co-defendants. I asked him why he allowed his daughter to become close to a man that we both knew to be a villain. 'He is always nice to her – gives her sweets and that – you know.'

'That's not the point I'm making. I wouldn't want him near my daughter, however nice he is.'

He looked. 'I suppose this is the first lesson?'

'No, it's not. It's not a lesson at all, because you already know exactly what I mean.'

'I know you're right.'

He looked thoughtful. 'My son's hardly spoken to me!'

'Well, it's not surprising, is it? He hardly knows you – this is something for you to think about – it will take a lot of patience.'

Perhaps he had a conscience after all.

The next morning he reported at the office and brought his wife with him. We went through the official business as usual. He was very co-operative. 'You'll never have any trouble with me, Mr Mott.' And to be fair, I never did.

It had not escaped my notice that I was always 'Mr Mott', and he never attempted to discover my christian name. I thought that we had established a status quo.

On the occasion of this visit I noticed that his wife was now wearing two expensive diamond rings. He saw me looking at them.

'She had those rings in hock – that's how she managed to pay the bills.'

It was my turn to grin. 'You've only been out for twenty-four hours and she's got them back – how come?'

'I borrowed from friends.'

I bet you did.

In my subsequent interviews with him, I think I learnt as much as he did, if not more. He seemed to be repentant at times but I always knew there was more to him than he would admit. And yet he would sometimes be on the defensive, and in being so, would reveal further aspects of his personality . . .

One day . . . 'I'm not really as bad a man as you think, Mr Mott.'

'Oh, what makes you say that?'

'Well, that occasion when we beat up that bloke in the garage – it was me that called a taxi and gave the driver a tenner to take him to St Thomas's Hospital.'

'Because you were afraid of the consequences if he did not get treatment?'

'Not really – I felt sorry for him.'

In fact, this was the first I had heard of this incident, so once again, he was telling me something. We discussed his attitude toward crime and other criminals. He told me that he once shared a cell with Savundra, whom he thought was a real crook!

He also discussed sex crimes with some of the perpetrators whom he had met in the prison, in an effort to try and understand them. Brian was a very complex character indeed and I doubted if I was ever going to have any lasting effect upon him. And yet at times, when discussing his family and future, I had an odd feeling that I was getting to him.

He was living on social security, but he was a good car mechanic and was hoping to start a second-hand car business. One day he came into the office and asked me if he was allowed, under the terms of his licence, to go abroad. I told him he was allowed to go abroad for a maximum of twenty-one days, and if he stayed longer than that, the extra time could be added to his parole period. He then asked me if he could take the twenty-one days in weekends, and I told him that this was possible, providing that I approved of it.

'What is all this about?'

'I want to go to Holland for several weekends, so that I can buy second-hand cars there and import them to England for resale. Cars are cheaper over there and the tax is a lot less, so I should be able to make a fair profit on each.'

'I'm sorry, Brian, but it's not on. You were convicted of offences relating to imports, some of which have never been paid for or recovered. As you parole officer I cannot agree to it, and if you appeal to the Parole Board you are almost certain to be turned down.'

I was expecting a sharp reaction to this ruling, but I had underrated his own assessment of the situation. He had obviously expected that he would run into difficulty and thought it out.

'I can go for weekends, though? Without business ties?'

'Yes.'

'Good. I'll take my wife with me and she can do all the business. There's no law against that, is there?'

'No.'

'OK then, that's what we'll do.'

Now I was determined to keep one step ahead of him if I could, and as I knew nothing whatever about imports or exports, I decided to telephone the Board of Trade, and find out all I could. I did this and I spoke to a Board of Trade official for more than twenty minutes. At the end of the conversation I was wondering what this official actually got paid for, because he didn't seem to know any more about imports than I did, and I was certainly none the wiser for having spoken to him. I was determined to make it plain to Brian that I was keeping a check on his activities, so the next time he reported at the office I told him ... 'I phoned the Board of Trade this week Brian.'

'Oh, what did you do that for?'

'I wanted to know all there is to know about importing cars from Holland.'

'I see. What did they tell you?'

I had to grin when he asked me this. 'As a matter of fact, I spoke to an official for twenty minutes and he never told me a thing.'

It was his turn to grin. 'You should have asked me!'

He eventually managed to find a site with a small office

where he established a second-hand car sales business. I always knew that he was a deeper character than appeared on the surface, but it was really nothing more than suspicion and perhaps I was doing him an injustice. Anyway, he was working at his business without a hint of trouble. At last the time came for his licence to terminate, and as it turned out, for him to restore the status quo.

'I've booked a table for lunch at the local pub on the day after I finish parole. You've been the governor for twelve months, so now I'm taking you out to lunch and on that day I'll be the governor. OK?'

'OK.'

I went out to lunch with him and enjoyed it very much. We had a couple of brandies, which I paid for (status quo) in case the Home Office thought he was trying to get round me for a possible future occasion. Strangely enough, I felt there was not going to be a future occasion.

Later, when looking at the file, the Deputy Chief Probation Officer asked me: 'Do you think it was wise to go out to lunch with a man like this?'

I replied: 'If you don't believe that people can change, what are you doing in the Probation Service?'

About a year later, Brian's wife telephoned me.

'Mr Mott, Brian has been found dead in his office – it was his heart.'

I sat back in my chair and thought about him. Surely there are a lot of lessons to be learned when thinking about his life. In my mind there were two things that were fairly certain.

He wasn't all evil; but he wasn't a genius either.

☆ ☆ ☆

By contrast, Ken's was a more straightforward case. In comparison, he was not a sophisticated character or a professional criminal. He was, however, a very complex character who claimed to be a Jamaican, but with an undoubted oriental background. True, he was brought up in the West Indies and later came to England and became a merchant seaman. During his travels he met and later married a very attractive Italian girl who was as small and petite as he was large and tall. He committed offences, usually when he was short of money,

94

but soon got caught because they were impulsive offences, such as snatching cash from the Post Office counter and trying to run away. An accurate description of him was always enough to reveal his identity.

His wife was always furious with him when he made a fool of himself, leaving her to cope with two small children. She put forth her views in no uncertain terms and was in no way deterred by their difference in size.

Ken was a great sportsman and his greatest love in life was cricket, at which he excelled both as bowler and with the bat. This was to stand him in good stead when he found himself languishing in the security wing at Standford Hill Prison.

Now this prison could be described as being almost two prisons in one. Built on a hill, the lower part of the prison consisted of army-style huts and was a semi-open type of prison. But within these bounds was a block surrounded by high wire, with barbed wire on the top, and a separate gate by which to enter. Discipline in this block was firmer and security was a prime factor.

The senior officers were very keen on cricket, and there was a very nice cricket pitch in the lower part of the prison, where outside teams would sometimes play by invitation. I think Ken was probably put in the security block because of his habit of running away from the scene of the crime. Whatever the case, that's where he was when I first met him. When discussing his case at a later date, with a senior prison officer I happened to mention that Ken was an excellent cricketer and had almost become a professional when living in the West Indies. This seemed to spark some interest in his case.

Now, far be it from me to suggest that this had any bearings on the administration of the prison, but by some strange coincidence, the next time I visited him, he had been transferred to the lower part of the prison, and was therefore eligible for the cricket team!

He settled down well here, although his Italian wife never really understood the importance of cricket as part of his education and reform. Eventually, he was given a date of release and I realized that he would be given a hard time at home if he did not get down to some serious work and become the family breadwinner.

I had a friend at a large firm of Board Mills at Merton, and he was the Personnel Officer at the time. I contacted him and explained the situation with regard to Ken. He agreed to interview him and if he was suitable, would give him a job. After release, Ken duly went along there and was successful in getting a job. When I spoke to my friend later I was told that Ken was a very good worker and they were very pleased with him.

This had the effect of settling the family down, and they used to take the bat and ball into the park at weekends, and became a happy, close-knit family. He completed his term of licence satisfactorily and I had no further contact with him for over a year.

It so happened that another man was due to be released from prison, and as I had not contacted my friend the Personnel Officer for some time, I decided to try and get this latest client a job at the Mills. I telephoned him, but I was told: 'I am afraid he has left, Mr Mott, it is all different here now. It is all run by the Union, and the Union Secretary takes on the staff. He is in, if you'd like to talk to him – I'll put you through – his name is KEN!'

Needless to say, my new client got the job!

☆   ☆   ☆

Having just mentioned cricket, and football being my favourite sport, I recall the following . . .

I received the case history of a young man, aged twenty, who had just been sentenced to six months' imprisonment for fighting on the underground. As he was under the age of twenty-one when sentenced, he was at that time classified as a 'young prisoner' and was subject to a period of statutory after care. He was living with his grandmother, aged seventy-four, and there were just the two of them, because his grandfather had died, and his parents were separated. Both of them made alternative arrangements and were living elsewhere.

When he was sent to prison, his grandmother was most upset, and when I went to visit her she told me that his grandfather would have felt very badly about the whole thing, because he had taught the boy to play football and got him a trial for Crystal Palace, but after a while, he was released by the Club because it was thought that he might not make the grade as a professional footballer.

His grandmother told me that, when he was playing football, he was well disciplined and well-behaved, and it was only since he had left the 'Palace' that he had been mixing with the wrong type of company. As a result of this he began to stay out late and eventually got into the fight that resulted in his prison sentence.

She told me that she was hoping that after his release he would start playing football again. She was going to buy him a new pair of football boots, to encourage him, and she said she knew his size because they often wore each other's slippers, and he took the same size as her . . .

There was a shoe shop in Sutton that had a sale on, and in the window was a pair of football boots reduced to one pound. A seventy-four years old lady walked into the shop and told an astonished sales assistant: 'I would like to try those football boots on, please!' He got them out of the window, and slipping off her shoes, she tried them both on. 'They feel quite comfortable,' she said, stamping up and down the shop. 'Good, I'll take them.'

She paid her £1, leaving him scratching his head in amazement!

☆ ☆ ☆

A person who is serving a sentence of imprisonment for life, may, if it is thought appropriate, be released on licence, with the approval of the Home Secretary. That person will be under the jurisdiction of a parole officer for the following three years, but after that, will remain on licence for the rest of their life, unless terminated by the Home Office. Naturally, these are all serious cases and are treated as such within the Probation Service. Contact in such cases is usually made early, and the relevant documents relating to the case are received as soon after sentence as possible. The supervising officer in such cases is usually appointed by the senior probation officer, having regard to any special requirements that may be deemed advisable, but also, the nature of the offence. The supervising officer is likely to be well-versed in after care, and in some cases, could be the senior probation officer in person.

Apart from other considerations, a senior officer would not

wish to put a less experienced officer at risk. And this is something which is not impossible – and not to be taken lightly. In such cases, there exists a wider range of responsibility including a duty to the general public where a possible risk of further offences emerges.

I would like to refer to one such case, where these possibilities did emerge. But I hasten to add, in fairness to my client, that my anxiety was unfounded, and the case ended in a most satisfactory manner.

Malcolm was twenty years old, and came from a good family; nice parents and no hint of any previous trouble. He was well-behaved and had several interests, such as fishing, which he shared with his father.

Had he been less well-behaved, perhaps it would never have happened, but he did have a girlfriend – and he did cause her death. He was not the sort of youngster that had a lot of girlfriends, but she did have other boyfriends, and it later emerged that this caused him to worry excessively about her. Pressure of this kind, particularly in the young, is both hard to share – and also hard to bear.

In the end, something snapped, and he caused her death by stabbing her with a knife. He turned the knife upon himself, in his grief, but he recovered, and stood trial. At the age of twenty he was sentenced to life imprisonment.

I visited him in prison where I met him for the first time. Yes, he was remorseful, but resigned to his fate. He, like so many others, wished he could turn the clock back.

'It would never happen again.'

I was favourably impressed with him but the die was cast and he would have to make the best of his sentence.

He did just that. He studied engineering and while serving his sentence he passed two City and Guilds examinations. His image was excellent and he was a model prisoner. I mention this because I was surprised at a remark made to me by a senior prison officer who was on his wing. 'He's as good as gold – you'll get no trouble from him. I've tried to goad him and make him lose his temper, but he won't. He's all right.'

This gave me cause for thought . . . he had already killed somebody!!!

After serving nearly thirteen years the Home Secretary decided that he should be released upon licence. He returned to his parents' home, and the reunion was most successful, based on family ties. They had always stood by him and now was no exception. He had excellent qualifications and it was not long before he found a job and settled down.

He was amazed at the changes that had taken place outside, whilst he was in prison, and travelled around London looking at the different roads and buildings. The biggest change of all was the introduction of decimal currency, but he soon became accustomed to it, partly because there was some instruction about this within the prison.

We got on well together when I saw him, which was every week, until I suddenly had to go into hospital to have a hernia operation. I arranged for him to report to the Senior Probation Officer in my absence and there were no difficulties about his supervision.

Two weeks later, I was lying in bed in the local hospital with my wife and daughter at my bedside, when into the ward walked Malcolm. This was typical of him. It just a nice, friendly gesture, out of the goodness of his heart, and I appreciated it very much.

As a friend that is! For as a Probation Officer, I now had a client who had served a life sentence for causing a person's death, who now knew my wife and daughter. In my heart I knew that this would not become a major problem, but commonsense made me warn them both that, should he ever call at my home, he should not be allowed in. This was the sense of responsibility towards others that I mentioned earlier, and it would be most unwise to write it off.

Later, I refer to the possible dangers of the job, and I hope that what I have to say about that will show that extreme caution is sometimes not without justification. Happily, in this instance, my caution proved to be unnecessary, and we went on to share a trusting relationship.

After he had been home for about two years, he called to see me and told me that he had surprise for me. He told me that he was becoming engaged to be married. Once again there was food for thought in the role of parole officer. He was full of enthusiasm and told me a lot about her. We discussed the forthcoming wedding: 'In about six months', and all their plans but the vital question had to come.

'Malcolm, have you told her about your past – I mean, all of it?'

'No, not all of it.'

'Don't you think you owe it to her to know all about it, before she marries you? And even owe it to yourself? You see, you have set the stage to be very similar to that which existed fifteen years ago. I suggest that you clear the air, and when you do, remember that she *could* change her mind about the wedding. You have got to be prepared for that.'

'Yes, I know you're right – I knew I should have told her when I asked her to marry me, but I was afraid she might say no!'

'Can you handle it if she does?

He gave it some thought.

'I know what you mean, Mr Mott. Don't worry, I will tell her everything and if she changes her mind, I will walk away from it, there'll be no trouble.'

The following week, he came to my office in high spirits.

'I've told her everything, Mr Mott, and she was most understanding, we had a long talk and she's still going to marry me.'

'That's great – congratulations.'

He looked at me.

'Mr Mott?'

'Yes?'

'Thanks!'

I smiled at him. 'Bring her up to this office next week when you come, will you, Malcolm?'

'Of – yes – of course, you'd like to meet her.'

'You're sure you've told her everything?'

'Yes.'

'Good, because now I'm going to tell her!'

The following year they were married. The marriage almost coincided with the completion of his three years' reporting period on licence. In fact, there were just four weeks left when he moved to a different area to settle down to married life. I asked him to travel back to Sutton each week and report to me, and he was pleased to do so. That way, I did not have to transfer the case history to a local office – and they made a fresh start in life in a new area. Hopefully – all's well that ends well.

8

PRISON

There are other aspects of parole that are sometimes relevant, but not always apparent. Not least of these are the anxieties that are experienced by some prisoners who become eligible to apply for parole. I have met men who had become so paranoid about it, that they will not apply, for fear of getting a refusal. Some men find a great deal of difficulty in revealing their true feelings, and some interpretation is sometimes required.

For several years I acted in the role of Liaison Officer between the South West London Probation area and Standford Hill Prisoners. This entailed monthly visits to the prison, when I would interview all those prisoners whose home was within that probation area. This area included about half a dozen probation offices and I would contact the appropriate office each month, with a short report on each of their prospective clients. At that time I had a rather distinctive car, which was yellow with a black vinyl roof. I used to park this outside the welfare office, and it soon became known to most of the prison inmates – and staff too.

One day, I was about to leave the prison, but as I approached my car I saw a prisoner leaning against the driver's door. Two other prisoners were nearby, going through the motions of weeding the flower beds, but obviously aware that something was about to take place. As I approached this man said to me: 'Are you a parole officer, mate?'

I looked at him. 'Yes, I am in some cases.'

'I'm not putting in for it; I'm not having no probation officer going round to my house, knocking my missus off.'

'I see – have you got any children?'

'Yes, two, a boy and a girl, both at school.'

'And what are they living on?'

'My missus gets social security so she's all right.'

'You call trying to look after two children, and living on Social Security while their father is in prison, all right?'

There was no reply.

I said: 'Let's get it straight then – you are in an open prison, with three square meals a day – no rent to pay, and television available in the evenings, while she is struggling at home to keep your two kids on social security. And you're not going to apply for parole to at least try to get out and help them?'

Again, no reply, but there was now a different look on his face. The gardeners had stopped gardening, and were obviously listening. I got into my car and then put the window down. I told him: 'You've got one thing to be thankful for.'

'What's that?'

'I'm not *your* *** probation officer!'

Four weeks later I went back on my monthly visit, and I had really forgotten about this incident, but as I left to go home, there he was again, standing by my car door. As I approached he called out: 'I've put in for it.'

I grinned at him (no gardeners this time). 'That's good, I hope you're successful.'

'Do you think I'll get it?'

'I'm sorry, I don't know – I don't know about your case, but you must have a probation officer of your own.'

I got into the car and was about to drive away when he knocked on the window. I put the window down. 'Thanks mate!'

I never saw him again.

In contrast, I was actually in the prison recreation centre when a prisoner came over to me and said: 'You're a probation officer, aren't you?'

I told him that I was.

'My probation officer is no *** good!'

'Isn't he? Perhaps he thinks you're no *** good. After all, you're in here and he's outside.'

I looked at him. 'Why do you come up to me to tell me that your P.O. is no good?'

'Well, he never comes to see me.'

'Ah, are you trying to tell me that you would like to see him?'

'I wouldn't mind.'

'OK. You tell me who he is and I'll phone him tomorrow and tell him I've seen you. Oh, and I'll need your name.'

The next day I telephoned a colleague at Chatham and explained what had occurred.

'We've been so busy here. I've felt guilty about not visiting him, but we're snowed under . . . I'll try and go next week, and thanks.'

If only there were more days in a Probation Officer's week . . .

☆ ☆ ☆

One of my colleagues – a prison welfare officer – was a really nice chap but inclined to be somewhat over-protective to visiting probation officers. I arrived at the prison one day, to find him hopping about like a cat on hot bricks. He couldn't wait for me to get into the Welfare Office before pouncing on me.

'I must see you about Gonzales, he said, full of anxiety.

'Whose Gonzales?' I asked.

'He's an arch con man – he'll twist you round his little finger – don't believe a word he tells you.'

I was grateful for his warning but having now been a probation officer for over twenty years, I thought I might be trusted to make up my own mind. Nonetheless he hovered around me until Mr Gonzales was escorted to the welfare office.

Well, he certainly lived up to the reputation of Speedy Gonzales in appearance. Flashing eyes, good-looking, with a pencil moustache and dazzling white teeth. All this backed by a charming smile and a soft voice.

My colleague was fussing about like a mother hen when Gonzales and I went into an office and closed the door on him. Half an hour later, at the end of the interview, I opened the door and he was still there.

'How did you get on?' he asked me, his voice full of anxiety.

'I thought he was absolutely charming. He sold me a carpet!'

☆ ☆ ☆

I went to Maidstone Prison to visit a possible parolee, but first I wanted to discuss the case with that grand, stalwart, welfare officer, Joe Nixon. I was told that he was not in his office, but was somewhere in the prison. One of the prison officers called over a 'trusty' prisoner, wearing a blue armband.

'Take Mr Mott round the prison, and find Mr Nixon, will you?'

'Yes, sir, will you come this way sir?'

As we walked across the prison yard he remarked: 'A lovely day, sir?'

'I said: 'Yes,' thinking that he was quite a pleasant little fellow.

I wondered what he had done.

'Ah well,' said he. 'I've nearly finished my sentence and then I'll be able to go out on a day like this.'

'That's nice,' I said. 'You're due for release soon?'

'Yes. Only another four years!'

Now I really was wondering what he had done, but it is not always expedient to ask.

At that point I saw Joe across the prison yard. I pointed him out to my 'trusty' friend and he said: 'Oh, you know him, sir? I need not come any further then?'

I thanked him for escorting me, and when he went back, I couldn't help thinking how polite and helpful he had been.

When I approached Joe Nixon, he was standing there grinning at me; probably noticing the questioning look on my face.

'You know who that was, don't you?'

'No.'

'That was Vassall!'

There was another unusual happening that day.

I had met the man I was visiting on several occasions before. In fact, I had prepared reports for the Court at the time of his sentence. It was a serious offence of burning a man with acid, and a prison sentence had been inevitable. I had given him quite a lot of support in the past, so I was quite surprised when I was told he didn't want to see me.

'In that case, please tell him that *I* want to see *him*!'

I was eventually led to a side room apart from the usual offices, and there I found him in a state of extreme anxiety. It was obvious that there was something really wrong.

'It's nothing to do with you Mr Mott, but the officers' mess canteen was broken into a few days ago, and they haven't found out who did it. If I see you today, and then they find out who did it, they might think I have "grassed" on them. They'll half kill me.'

I told him: 'Your best plan is to forget about it. Your very attitude and state of anxiety tells me that you know who did it, so let's forget it. I actually came here to discuss . . .'

Such is prison life – wheels within wheels.

I visited another prisoner on three or four occasions, on behalf of a fellow officer at Kingston. He and his brother-in-law had committed a burglary in that area, but only he had been caught. His brother-in-law, according to him, had got away with it. The first time that I saw him we had a fairly general discussion, but he did ask me to get a message to his wife. It concerned an old car that he said was parked outside his house. Under no circumstances was she to get rid of this car, even though it was not in very good condition, not taxed, and not insured. I asked him if it was wise to hang on to it, but he said he wanted to work on it when he came out. The second time I visited him, he immediately asked about his car, and I told him that as far as I knew, the car was still there. He seemed to be quite relieved about this, and again stressed that she was not to get rid of it. His anxiety was beginning to give me food for thought.

The third time I visited him he, once again, asked anxiously about his car, but this time, with a slight amendment. 'Tell her, under no circumstances, to let me brother-in-law have it.'

I asked him if he realized that, if it was in the poor condition which he described, it might be in danger of being towed away. He broke down, and told me that the money they had stolen had never been recovered; it was hidden in the spare tyre of the car.

I told him that I was now dutybound to report this to the Kingston police, and he agreed.

'As long as my brother-in-law doesn't get it!'

I telephoned Kingston police later, and a couple of days later, they phoned back. Sure enough, the stolen money was recovered.

I didn't mention the brother-in-law.

☆　☆　☆

The jobs of prison officers, probation officers and police officers, seem to me to offer interesting comparisons. On the surface, each of these vocations are completely different, and in my experience, the characters and personalities that they involve are also totally different. Certainly, I have not met many probation officers that might, in my opinion, excel as prison officers, although quite a number of my colleagues have shown a preference, and an aptitude, for the role of prison welfare officer. I also know several ex-police officers who have eventually joined the probation service, and been extremely successful.

I would suggest, however, that they are the exception rather than the rule. I have always been of the opinion that the task of prison officer is the most difficult of all. Those that I have met personally have, mostly regarded their job as a vocation in which they feel that they are serving the general public, and at the same time, fulfilling an important role in the maintenance of law and order.

A few years ago, when the more severe discipline was established in some selected Detention Centres, an officer at Send remarked to me:

'Do you think that they are going to turn us into tyrants overnight?'

There is compassion in each of these jobs, backed by the belief that, at the end of the day, somebody, somewhere, has benefited by our efforts. Why, then, the comparisons?

Each of these services are, within a little, dealing with the same clients. But we look at the same people through different eyes, and we are each looking for something different. Each of us is obliged to do the job for which we were selected and trained, and we do have to respect each other, and the part we have to play.

The following may help to demonstrate my meaning:

I was visiting a prisoner at Standford Hill, who had several previous convictions for petty offences. He had a wife and two little girls who lived in a house in Surrey. During our discussions he told me that, although he and his wife loved each other, she had told him that she was fed up with him and his way of life. The police were always knocking at the door, and she wanted her daughters to be brought up in a respectable manner. Because of this, she told him that he could find

106

somewhere else to live after his release, because she was not prepared to stand for it any longer. Now, there were two things in this case that I thought were worth noting. His date of release was about two weeks before Christmas, and also while in prison, he was making two dolls. It seemed obvious that as soon as he left the prison, he would want to see his daughters, and the dolls were going to be Christmas presents. When I asked him about this he revealed that, while what I suggested was true, he had some anxieties about the reception – or otherwise – that his wife might offer him. She had refused to visit him or bring the children, but she had written to tell him that they sent their love, etc. I suggested that I would contact the local probation officer in Surrey and ask him to visit her and discuss the whole situation. We might then be in a position to make some positive arrangements about the future. Eventually, both parties agreed to this, and after I had explained everything to the Probation Officer, and he had contacted her, it was further agreed that he would escort her to the prison, and we would have a meeting to examine the possibilities of a reconciliation.

Prior to this meeting, my prisoner began to become quite nervous about the outcome, but he undoubtedly loved his wife and kids, and wanted to return home.

It turned out to be a very successful meeting – eventually with a few tears and some kisses, etc.

We left them alone for a while, and when she left, it was with the understanding that my Surrey colleague would keep a close eye on things and give all the help he could. When December came, he was still in a state of anxiety because he had some lingering doubts if all would be well. In the end, it seemed to be working well, and after his release he returned home, where his Surrey Probation Officer had a job lined up for him.

While serving his sentence he had got on very well with a prison officer who originally came from Sunderland. He was a caring officer who, in spite of the disciplinary role, was interested in the prisoners under his jurisdiction and was always prepared to help them if he could.

On my next visit to the prison, I met this officer, who stopped me and told me: 'I will never help another bloody prisoner as long as I live.' I asked him what was wrong. 'That bastard – he told me that he would never go back to Surrey. He was finished with his wife and kids, and he was going up North to make a fresh start. I've got relations up in Sunderland, and I contacted them and arranged for him to have room, and they were going to help him find a job. I had it all arranged, and as soon as he came out the bastard went back to his wife and kids in Surrey. I'll never help another prisoner as long as I live.'

I was, of course, sympathetic.

The prisoner may have been looking for alternative accommodation, but I think it was far more likely that he was seeking reassurance. I doubt if he wanted or intended to go to Sunderland. He needed to be convinced that his rightful place was at home with his family. That should have been the course of action that this well-meaning officer pursued.

☆   ☆   ☆

YOU CAN'T MAKE A SILK PURSE OUT OF A SOW'S EAR – but don't stop trying. The end-product may not be a silk purse, but it might be something a lot better than a sow's ear.

When I used to visit men in the security wing at Standford Hill, I sometimes had the use of a tiny office which was otherwise used only by the 'trusty' as a part of his privilege. He was not a client of mine, so I had no knowledge of his record or background. He gave me the impression that he was no stranger to prison, and he certainly had a 'hard' look about his face. He was usually there when I visited, and we used to pass the time of day, but other than that I saw very little of him. One day, however, I was surprised to find a very ruffled-looking pigeon, sitting huddled on a roughly made perch in the corner. It had some water and some pieces of bread.

I asked him where it had come from. He told me that he had come upon it on the perimeter, tangled in the barbed wire, and had managed to disentangle it, only to discover that it had a jagged tear down the middle of its breast. He said that he had brought it into the office, and sewn it up! He picked up the pigeon and showed me the stitches down its 'middle'. I asked him how on earth he had managed to do it, and I felt quite sick when he explained. He had actually laid it on its back on the table, and then spread its wings out, which he held down by putting a pile of books on each wing. He had then sewn up the wound with an ordinary needle and cotton, and without any form of anaesthetic or painkiller! In a way, I was appalled at the very thought of this, but, thinking about it, there were several interesting aspects of his actions.

The first was, that a man of his character could have the compassion to attempt to save the pigeon's life, instead of wringing its neck, as some seemingly more compassionate people may have done. Secondly, the method which he used, given that prison facilities are not usually geared to operations on birds, how many of us could have carried out this operation, literally, in cold blood. Thirdly, whatever you may think of that, the fact remained that the pigeon was still alive, albeit looking quite a bit the worse for wear. He told me that he hoped that it would improve, and become more lively. He cleaned the wound each day with Jeyes Fluid and he had every hope that the bird would pull through. He said that he intended to remove the stitches, using the books as before.

I could not help feeling that this could be the only good that this man had done in his life. He was certainly anxious about the bird, and cared for it, in an offhand sort of way, almost as though it had a duty to him to recover.

About three weeks later, I went to the prison again, and this time, there was the pigeon, hopping and cooing, and seemingly in fine fettle. Furthermore, it now had a much improved perch which he had made out of some old wood, and there could be no doubt that he had actually saved this pigeon's life. He showed me the scar which was beginning to become covered with down, and some slight marks remaining after he had removed the stitches. I was genuinely delighted, more for the man than the pigeon, for, whatever his past, he obviously believed that he had done something to be proud of.

A month later, I visited the prison again, and whilst on my way, I found myself wondering about the pigeon. What a great moment, I thought to myself, for that man to cast the pigeon off and watch it soar heavenwards. Surely that would have some lasting effect upon him, perhaps for the good. I arrived at the prison and went to the tiny office. He was sitting at the table, and the pigeon was gone. No sign of the perch, nor breadcrumbs either. What about the pigeon? I asked him eagerly. He looked at me with the same hard look that I had noticed when we first met.

'It's gone – two *** screws took it out and let it go when I was on duty elsewhere – I never saw it go. And the bastards wonder why we hate their guts.'

I will not be drawn into arguments about the rights or wrongs of that case, but it seemed to me to be a great opportunity missed. Perhaps it reflects the words that a Wandsworth Prison Officer said to me many years ago.

'Any one of these men may stab me in the back, and I have to treat them all as though he's the one.'

This opinion does not seem to be borne out by the relationships that exist in most prisons between officers and men. There are a great variety of projects, both educational and physical, which are organized by enthusiastic officers in their vocation. The odd incident, which I have referred to here, does occur, but with a little better understanding might have been dealt with in a different way.

9

THE POLICE

Police Sergeant Arthur Pendlington was the Warrant Officer at the South Western Magistrates Court, when I arrived there, completely inexperienced, straight from the selection board. I was taken around the Court, and was introduced to the staff in each department. Everybody there worked well together, and I received a great deal of help and advice from the 'ground floor'.

I had been there for about two weeks, sharing an office with Barry Swinney, when, one day, I was sitting behind my desk writing a report, and the door was literally banged open and a very aggressive man charged in.

'Where's Swinney?' he shouted.

I explained to him that Mr Swinney would not be in the office that day as he was visiting a prison. The man then sat down on a chair and folded his arms.

'I'm not moving from here till I see him!'

Now, two weeks in the probation service does not actually prepare you to deal with this type of aggressive character. As a matter of fact, in my training so far, nobody had mentioned that this sort of thing can happen. I was just wondering what sort of action to take, when there was a tap at the door.

Without waiting for me to say 'Come in', the door opened, and in walked Arthur Pendlington.

'Mr Mott, I believe Mr Swinney is not in today, is that right?'

I was looking at our aggressive friend who seemed to have become a little bit agitated – he was looking from me to Arthur – and back.

'That is so, Sergeant. Can I help you in any way?'

'Ah yes, we could have a chat – is this gentleman just

leaving?'

'Well, he wanted Barry as well, but I have just explained to him that Mr Swinney is not here today.'

Sergeant Pendlington walked across to the man in the chair and said: 'In that case, Pat, you'll be going – right?'

'Oh yes, all right. Will he be here tomorrow?'

'Yes, I think so.'

'OK. I'll come back tomorrow.'

He got up and left – a lot more quietly than he had come in.

Arthur told me: 'That's Pat . . . He's a nasty bit of work, did you get any trouble with him?'

'No, thanks to you. You don't really want to see me, do you?'

He grinned. 'No, I saw him coming in and I knew you were on your own. I guessed that he might cause trouble. You'll be all right now. He won't come back.'

He went over to the door and looked back and grinned again. We were friends, until the day that he retired from the force to become a taxi driver.

Thanks, Arthur.

At about the same time that this happened I was Court Duty Officer when two men appeared charged with assaulting a police officer. I have met many police officers since, but none that have been a better example of a dedicated officer. He was a young constable, aged about twenty-two, and he was standing in the doorway at about midnight on his beat. There was snow on the ground, and as he stood there, out of sight, two men, who seemed to have had a few drinks, came along the road. One of them was carrying a shovel, and the other was bowling snowballs, which the one with the shovel was hitting. In short, playing cricket in the snow. This, in itself, was fairly harmless, until, tiring of the game, they began to try the door handles of cars. When they actually managed to open a car door, the constable went over to them, only to be immediately punched in the face by one of these men. The pavement was slippery, and the blow dislodged his helmet, which fell off. He fell to the ground, but in doing so he managed to grab the leg of the man that had hit him. The other man hit him on the head with the shovel, but still he held on.

He held on to that man's leg, in spite of repeated blows to the head and body, with the shovel, until he eventually lost

112

consciousness. Only then did that man free himself. Luckily, other officers arrived on the scene, and the two assailants were quickly apprehended.

Listening to the evidence in that case left with me a lasting impression about devotion to duty. I did not always agree with everything the police said, or did, in the years to come, but I have never ceased to admire the courage of that young constable. His attackers were eventually committed to the high court, and, quite rightly, received heavy prison sentences.

The police, of course, don't always agree with all that a probation officer says, or does. As I have already said, we deal with mutual clients in different ways, depending on our position in the case. But perhaps I will leave the last word on this to my old friend, Detective Sergeant Tom Newbury, now retired but at one time a very active officer in South London. Tom was stationed at Earlsfield at the time, and he was the officer in a case in which I too was involved. We disagreed considerably when discussing the accused, who was known to both of us very well. The argument became quite heated and in the end we said some rather uncomplimentary things about each other's ancestors, and I stalked off upstairs to my office.

Ten minutes later there was a knock at my door and in walked Tom with his hand extended.

'We've been friends for too long to fall out over a bloody villain!'

We shook hands. There's a lesson to be learned there.

☆　☆　☆

There was a laundry in Battersea that was fairly busy and employed quite a number of local people. Unfortunately articles of clothing, sheets, pillowcases, towels etc., began to go missing on a fairly regular scale. It seemed obvious that these items were being taken by one of the employees, and a watch was kept by the management. After a while they felt that they had traced the culprit, but try as they might, they could not actually catch her red-handed. They decided to report it all to the police and let them deal with it. After investigation the police decided that the woman in question was undoubtedly Suspect Number one, but again, they could not actually catch her in the act. She was a married woman in her forties, living with her family in Wandsworth, and it was decided that the next time goods went missing, they could go to her house with a search warrant, in the hope of finding the stolen goods on her premises. One day, more goods disappeared, and the police duly descended upon the woman's home.

I am sure that it must have been entirely coincidental that the officer in charge of this raid was my detective friend from Hurley's bookshop. He, and other officers, arrived at the said address with their search warrant, announced that they were police officers, and then thoroughly searched the premises. Alas, they could find nothing that could have been stolen from the laundry and they were forced to leave empty-handed. My friend was an extremely nice man, and always polite. He got to the front door and turned and said to the woman: 'I'm awfully sorry, Mrs X, there seems to have been some mistake.'

'I ain't Mrs X – she lives next door!'

Oh dear!

On another occasion, a young married woman telephoned me and asked if she could call and see me about some trouble she was having with her husband. We made an appointment, and later that week she called at my office. She lived with her husband and two small children in a house in Putney, and I soon realized that both her husband and her brother were known to me because of offences usually involving aggression and violence. This woman was obviously very much in fear of her husband, and told me that he would often use violence against her, but he was fond of the children, and so far, had never hurt them.

A few months ago she had met a man she used to go out with before she was married. Foolishly she had agreed to meet him for a drink, and they had gone to a local pub. This had been discovered by her husband, and he had given her a good hiding. Now he was attempting to find the man whom she had met and was threatening to beat him up. Usually, on such occasions, his brother would join in, and the situation could become quite nasty.

It became even more complicated when she told me the name of her 'boyfriend', who was about a foot taller than her husband, and also known to the probation service for offences of violence. I didn't dare try to visualize what might happen if ever the two were to meet. She told me that she had known

114

that I knew her husband in the past, and hoped that I might speak to him, and convince him that there was nothing whatever in her relationship with the other man. Knowing her husband, this was going to be easier said than done, but I did agree to telephone him and invite him to my office to discuss the situation. She was suitably grateful and breathed a sigh of relief. Like so many big, aggressive men, they often have a likeable side to their character, but are completely different when they become upset. I thought that this was a fairly accurate assessment of his personality, but later events seemed to show that my judgement was considerably at fault.

I telephoned him and told him that his wife was worried because she had upset him, and there seemed to be no real reason for him to be upset. I suggested that he might call at my office and see me, and we could discuss the situation. He told me that he was working on a building site in Putney, and would find it difficult to get to Lavender Hill, but he could nip home in the afternoon. I could call in for a cup of tea and we could talk about it then. This seemed to be a reasonable arrangement, and I agreed to call the following day. The next day I called at the house as arranged, and he was already there. His wife was also there, and after saying hello, she went into the kitchen to make the tea, and he asked me to go into the front room, where he showed me into an armchair. He sat across the room on the settee, and I began to get an uneasy feeling that something was not quite right about this visit.

His wife came in with the tea, and then sat down in the other armchair. I was watching him closely, and he was undoubtedly becoming agitated. There was a few moments silence, and then he pulled out a large jack-knife which was already open, and had been concealed at the back of the settee. He held it up in a threatening manner and said: 'The first one to move gets this!'

I looked across at his wife. She seemed to be petrified, and I knew that, if anybody was going to handle this situation, it had to be me. I sat still, but my mind was working overtime. I thought that this was a situation in which earlier advice might stand me in good stead: 'When in doubt, do nowt' or 'do what you believe to be right'. In this case it may have to be a little of each. But one thing I did know. I had to get possession of that knife. In addition to it being an offensive weapon, it was also something for him to hide behind. The question was, was he too disturbed to listen to reason, and what was he hoping to achieve?

I could not hope to take it from him, and to try to do so could have disastrous results. I decided to wait a while and see what developed. He was glaring across at his wife, and said: 'I want to know the name of this bloke you've been having it off with.'

I told him: 'We agreed that I should come round and discuss what happened. Your wife came to my office to ask me to explain to you that nothing at all happened. She came to my office to ask me that, because you won't listen to her. She made a mistake and she admits it, and I'm sorry that I came here, not because you've got the knife, but because I think it's a bloody waste of my time trying to talk to you.'

I held my breath.

'I just want his name, that's all. I'm not having him coming round here when I'm at work. I want to see him.'

'Do you love her?'

There was a hint of a tear in his eye. 'She knows I do.'

She was now curled up in the armchair, quietly sobbing.

'I'll tell you what I'll do – I'll leave you now, and perhaps you can tell her that when I'm not here. If you really love her you've got to trust her – and accept her apology.'

I stood up – this was it!

'There is one thing though – if I leave here now, I'm taking that knife with me. I don't want you to do something that you will be sorry for.'

I held out my hand, and looked him straight in the eye. He folded the knife and handed it to me, and I walked toward the door. I gave him a sign to come to the front door with me, which he did. I asked: 'Are you going back to work?'

'Later, yes.'

'Give her a kiss before you go – she's more than paid for one small indiscretion.'

He nodded – he was much calmer now. I felt that I could safely leave her, and the children would soon be home. There was no likelihood of violence towards them.

We shook hands and he said: 'I'm sorry about that.'

I left, but I was far from happy about the situation, which was really no nearer to an amicable reunion. At least I had got that knife out of the house, and perhaps relieved the situation for the time being, but what of the future? When I got back to my office, I telephoned the house, and she answered. He had gone back to work and the children were at home. She said that he often gets upset but he has never used a knife before. I told her that she must try and contact the police if there is any future behaviour that may lead to an assault or worse. I gave the matter a great deal of thought, and I couldn't really make up my mind what, if anything, to do.

I didn't know then, that my mind was about to be made up for me.

The next afternoon I received a telephone call from Putney Police Station; it was Chief Superintendent Peter Vibart. He said that he believed that I had been in touch with Bill X recently, was that correct?

I said that it was, and I outlined the events of the last few days. Peter Vibart was a first-class copper of the old school, who didn't mince words. 'You took a knife off him?' I admitted that I had. 'You were *** lucky – he sounds like a nutcase.'

'Would you mind telling me what has happened now, then?'

'He's taken his two children and disappeared with them. He was last seen walking with them on the towpath by the river at Putney. His wife has been here, and is desperately afraid that he may do them some harm – what do you think?'

'In the ordinary way, I don't think he would actually harm them, but he was very disturbed yesterday and if he has had a mental breakdown, anything could happen.'

'That's what I think. The safety of the children is of paramount importance. We are doing all we can and we are considering putting their pictures on television.'

'Is there anything I can do?'

'There might be. His wife told us that he liked you and it is possible that you will be the only link between him and us or his wife. We have put her in a "safe house" with a friend, so he can't contact her directly, so he may try to contact you. I've got a bright young copper who will be watching you for the next few days, and if Bill X contacts you in any way you must let my man know immediately. OK?'

That was how I first met Detective Constable John Pole, who later in his career rose to a much more exalted position.

I suddenly became aware that he was shadowing me every-where I went, and I invited him into my office to discuss a method of working. We agreed that, when I was working in my office he could have the use of the office next door, and by experimenting, we discovered that by banging on the wall I could alert him if required. At times when I was out or in Court, he would follow at a discreet distance. We did this for the next few days, and in that time there was no sign of Bill and the children, in spite of rigorous efforts to trace them.

Then the telephone rang, and when I answered it, it was Bill speaking. At this moment I was supposed to bang on the wall, and D.C. Pole would come rushing in and take over, possibly to try and trace the call or whatever police officers do under these circumstances. But Bill, suddenly reverted to being my probation client and in spite of the fact that I was worried about the children, I did not, at that moment, bang on the wall – instead I greeted him fairly affably then: 'What can I do for you?'

'Can we meet somewhere, Mr Mott?'

'I'm sorry, Bill, but I'm not prepared to do that at the moment, besides I am too busy. If you would like to see me you can come to my office.'

'Will you have me arrested?'

'Arrested, Bill? Why, what have you done?'

'I haven't done anything but I know the police are looking for me because of the children.'

'What about the children, are they all right?'

'Of course they're all right, you know I wouldn't harm the children. They're staying with friends and are being well looked after.'

'Look, Bill, come up here and talk to me, and I'll tell you now that there is a police officer waiting to interview you about the welfare of the children. If they are being well looked after, you have not committed any offence, because you are their legal guardian, but you have caused a lot of people a great deal of trouble. You'd better come up here and we'll try and sort it out.'

'I'll be there in half an hour Mr Mott.' At this point I hung up the telephone, and banged on the wall. Within seconds D.C. Pole came into my office looking expectant and seemed perplexed when he saw that I was alone.

'What's happened?' he asked.

I explained to him what had happened and said that I could

not bring myself to bang on the wall earlier. I told him that Bill would be coming to the office shortly, and I would introduce them.

'Have you phoned Vibart?' he asked.

'No, I haven't.'

'Well you'd better bloody well do it – I'm not going to do it – he'll have a bloody fit.'

He did – well, nearly.

I phoned him and told him what had happened, and in his gravel voice he asked if Pole had traced the call, or spoken to Bill. When I told him that I had not banged on the wall, there was a snort, followed by a minute's silence and then . . . 'You'd be no *** good as a copper!'

'Well, Mr Vibart, I don't think that you would be much good as a probation officer!'

'No – Every man to his own trade!'

☆   ☆   ☆

Bill came into the office as arranged, and I introduced him to D.C. Pole, in a very civilized fashion. He told us that, after the knife incident, his wife had threatened to leave him, and he really took the children to make sure she didn't go. We couldn't understand the logic of this, but people under stress often react in unpredictable ways. Bill agreed to come with us to Putney Police Station, and I must confess to a certain feeling of satisfaction when we walked into Peter Vibart's office.

But Peter was a true blue copper right down the line, and after listening to all that Bill had to say, he asked him to agree to a psychiatric examination, to be on the safe side. By now, Bill was ready to agree to anything and Mr Vibart got the duly authorized officer to make a seventy-two hours' order committing him to a mental hospital at Epsom for a check. All these preparations were already in hand, and I was most impressed by the thoroughness of the arrangements. Within the next few days Bill returned home with a clean bill of health. The children had been reunited with their mother, and she had visited him in hospital. They agreed to try and make a fresh start, and as an act of good faith, she even told him the name of the man that she had a drink with.

Bill just had to go and see this man, to satisfy his own ego. He

119

actually called at the man's house and introduced himself, but found himself face to face with a similar character to himself – only bigger. They decided to go and have a drink together, and talk it over, and they went to the same pub where the whole bloody thing had started in the first place!

If, as I hope, there are lessons to be learned, in each of the situations that I have related, then surely the biggest lesson here lies in the fact that, but for human reaction and inability to cope – none of this needed to happen at all. But isn't that the way with so many of our cases?

☆　☆　☆

Because it is my intention to give a straightforward and accurate account of experiences that may have to be faced, even though they are not very pleasant, here are two cases from which I derived no pleasure at all.

The first was a young colleague, who trained with me and who seemed to have a very promising future in the probation service. We became friendly, and we studied together, exchanging books and discussing ideas. Imagine the shock, when I learned that he had appeared at Tower Bridge Magistrates Court, charged with sexual offences against the son of his landlady. He was found guilty, and as a result of this offence was, rightly, dismissed from the probation service. The feeling within the service, if such an incident occurs, is one of sadness and compassion.

In the other case, I was called upon to prepare a social enquiry report on an ex-police constable who had been invalided out of the police force after twenty-four years' devoted service.

He had become involved in the running of a nightclub, and had allowed his name to be used in the application for a licence, obviously because he presented an acceptable image. Unfortunately, there were certain activities going on in the back room which resulted in a police raid, and several charges.

I felt extremely sad when I interviewed him, because I could imagine that he had given twenty-four years' of his life serving the public, and whatever indiscretions that he may have committed, I had no doubt that the good he had done in his life, far outweighed the bad.

I was obliged to present an unbiased, objective report to the court and I make no apology if I put the emphasis upon his past excellent record. He was given a suspended prison sentence. There are certain aspects involved in preparing a report of this kind which make the task extremely unpleasant. Happily, these cases seldom occur.

10

IN COURT

Who said I'm a criminal?
Who said I'm a crook?
Get yourself a looking glass,
And take a long, hard look.
You sit in judgement over me
But aren't you human too?
Don't you ever do the things
That other humans do?

One of the most serious, and sometimes heart-rending tasks undertaken by the probation service, is that of providing reports in matrimonial cases.

In such cases, the officer involved in the case is known as the Court Welfare Officer, and the reports are classed as Welfare Officer's reports as opposed to social enquiry reports, which may infer that some kind of offence has been committed. The Domestic Courts are civil courts with jurisdiction over separation and/or divorce cases and all that they entail, including custody and access of children, maintenance and other settlements.

The Welfare Officers are usually trained probation officers who are assigned to the domestic court, particularly in divorce cases, but as matrimonial cases may be heard at a magistrates (domestic) court, local officers often become involved in providing welfare reports.

This is a highly skilled job, with the future of individuals, or even whole families, dependent on the accuracy and reliability of the content of the report. The officers involved in preparing such reports are well aware of the responsibilities which they are expected to bear and it is absolutely essential that they exercise the utmost objectivity when interviewing all parties concerned, and, in particular, when interviewing children.

Even when the preparation of such reports seem to be straightforward as far as the court is concerned, there is often a lot of heartache and suffering, and even deeper, long-term emotional effects, to members of the family. There can be no winners, and in some cases, not even a really satisfactory settlement or agreement. In such cases, the welfare officer may have to make recommendations that are the best that can be suggested under difficult circumstances, and yet not wholly satisfactory to all parties.

At the end of the day, it is the court that will make the final decision, but the Welfare Officer's report often contains vital information – and possibly suggestions – that are important factors which the court considers before reaching a conclusion.

The job is sometimes made doubly difficult because the Welfare Officer is dealing with people who are already under stress, and the very presence of the officer sometimes brings forth unexpected reactions. Diplomacy is the order of the day, and the officer should try to instil confidence in the client that, whatever the content of the report, it will be impartial and in the best interests of all concerned. I would sometimes call at an address, at unusual times, with the object of making a firm appointment. This was a 'ploy' that brought forth differing receptions, sometimes most interesting.

I remember seeing a little boy aged four, who had been taken into the care of the local council, when his mother was alleged to have attempted to poison his father. He was living with foster parents, but he was showing all the symptoms of disturbance – scratching himself with pins, pulling faces, etc. When I saw him I felt that he was emotionally disturbed because he was missing the love and affection of his mother, however good the foster parents may have been. Eventually the charge of attempted murder had been dropped, and substituted for one of: 'Administering a noxious substance', and after a somewhat theatrical barrister had proved that Ajax in coffee may be unpalatable, but is actually harmless (he actually drank some in Court), this case was dismissed. It so happened that I passed the mother's flat each day, on my way to my office, so, at about nine fifteen am I called there to make a more convenient appointment. She had been expecting me to call on her at some time, and invited me to come in. 'Would you like a cup of tea?'

We went into the kitchen, and while she was making the tea she told me that she loved her little boy, and couldn't wait to get him back. What she had done was all in the heat of the moment, and now it was all behind her.

Her ex-husband was not asking for custody of the boy, and it was part of my job to try and estimate if, under the circumstances, the child would be well cared for. She showed me round the flat, and pointed out the little room that the boy would occupy, but there was one room that she didn't show me. We went back into the kitchen and she assured me that she lived here alone, and that there was plenty of room for her and her little boy. On the draining board there were two cups, two saucers, two plates etc. I got up and went to the door of the room that she had not shown me.

'Do you mind if I look in here?'

I opened the door, and discovered a man lying in the double bed. He looked at me. 'It's nothing to do with me, mate,' he said.

'Well, that depends.' I told them both. 'Look, I know that you have to have a private life, and I don't blame you for it, but a lot will depend on the actual situation. If you are going to tell me that this is a "one-night stand" – that you went out together last night and there's no future in it – in that case I will close the door and forget I've seen you. But if it is to be on a more permanent basis, such as getting married at a later date, then you will be very much involved with the little boy. If that is the case, then I think we should talk.'

'To be honest, I am living here and we do hope to get married eventually, but she thought that they wouldn't let her have her son back if you found out.'

'Let us make an appointment for me to call again at a more convenient time and then I can discuss it with you both.'

In fact, there proved to be a far more stable background to the situation with them living together, and after the case was heard she was reunited with her son. The only reason that she had attempted to conceal the actual background of her new life was one of anxiety and not really an attempt to be devious. Everybody is entitled to a private life, and even if this had been a less permanent relationship, the love and care that she could give to her son would probably have been a lot better than the existing arrangements. Conventional visits do not always bring out the true facts, and yet they are always more helpful than pretence.

☆　☆　☆

The saying: 'your client chooses you', is never more true than when dealing with children. When they are very young, their feelings – anxieties – emotions, are sometimes impossible to put into words, and to attempt to try and discuss them might be courting disaster. But a child can tell you a great deal by behaviour and reaction, and a little applied psychology may be quite rewarding. I once called to see a lady at her home to discuss domestic matters. She showed me in to the front room where there was a large parrot on a perch.

I sat on the extreme left side of the settee, and the lady sat in an armchair opposite. We were having a quiet conversation, when her little girl, aged four, came into the room. She said nothing, but she began – shyly – to dance. She was glancing at me, and was obviously reacting to my presence, as children do. I took no apparent notice of her, and went on talking to her mother. She left the room, and came back with a teddy bear, which she held up in front of me. I leaned over and whispered in her ear: 'What's his name?'

She came close and whispered in my ear: 'Teddy.'

Mother was about to chide her but I signalled to her to leave it. The little girl left the room. A few minutes later she returned with an armful of dolls, which she sat in a semicircle around my feet. She was looking at me, but said nothing.

We went on talking.

She left the dolls, and climbed on to the extreme right-hand seat of the settee. We went on talking. Now she was on the middle seat of the settee. Gradually she sidled along until now she was sitting beside me. Again, I signalled to the mother to say nothing.

Suddenly the child climbed on to my lap; she looked a little bit apprehensive, in case I objected. When I did not object, she settled on to my lap and closed her eyes.

'Why?'

I was a total stranger. I had never seen her before, but here

125

she was choosing me as a father figure. At that stage I did not know why, but I knew she had told me enough to give me good cause for thought.

This little girl lacked paternal affection but that was not to say that he was not a good father in the material sense. What she had done to me, she really wanted to do to him, but he did not realize it. Later, when I was shown round the house, I was surprised to find that the back garden was a complete aviary, with various varieties of birds, in several cages, that he been built by dad. Without realizing it, he looked after them all with care and affection, but left out the prettiest little bird of all.

☆ ☆ ☆

Sometimes it can go much deeper than that, and give cause for a great deal of anxiety. As in the case of the little girl, aged five, who was obliged to spend the whole of each alternative Sunday with her father, who was living with another woman. It can be most distressing for all concerned when 'the rules' have to be adhered to, particularly when the child does not want to go. This child painted red spots on her face to pretend that she had measles, so that she might be allowed to stay at home.

Unfortunately, separated parents do not often retain a relationship which allows them to discuss such a situation sensibly, and the Welfare Officer sometimes becomes involved in an almost impossible situation. When that happens, it is not a good idea to allow oneself to become 'piggy in the middle'. I remember a case when both parents were living with somebody else when a divorce was granted. They had a little boy, who had stayed with his father, and in an effort to be fair, the court gave custody to the father, but ruled that he should deliver the child to his mother's flat every other weekend and pick him up on Sunday evening.

The relationship between these parents was appalling, and they could do nothing but row every time they met. The poor little chap was always in the middle, almost like the rope in a tug of war, and my phone never stopped ringing, with one or other of the parents phoning me to complain about the other. I eventually wrote to both of them and told them that I was no longer prepared to be involved in the case, and that they must try and resolve their differences themselves in the best interest of their son. Relationships, however, remained frigid until came the day when father delivered the lad to his mother one Friday night.

He would not go near the front door but would sit in his car and watch the boy ring the bell. When he was admitted, father would then drive home. Only, on this day, having delivered his son to his mother, the car wouldn't start. After attempting to get it going for nearly half an hour, without success, his ex-wife's boyfriend came out.

'Look, I'm a motor mechanic. Would you like me to get it going for you?'

Reluctantly, father agreed, and after about ten minutes the engine roared into life.

'Look, why don't you come in and wash your hands, and have a cup of tea?'

'Well, yes, OK. And thanks for getting it going for me.'

The two men went into the flat. They all had a cup of tea together, and: 'They all lived happily ever after' – to coin a phrase.

Could there possibly be a better illustration of the foolishness of some parents who find themselves in a similar situation, when just a little thought and commonsense can make life so much easier for all concerned?

There are times when a welfare officer can be placed in a difficult situation, particularly when, as a professional person, and a representative of the court acting in a privileged role, a situation arises which might be construed as a breach of that privilege. Once again the officer has to do that which they believe to be right – but sometimes there is very little choice.

☆ ☆ ☆

I was asked to prepare a welfare report on a child at a time when the father was serving a sentence in Wandsworth prison. I visited the mother and child at their flat in Richmond and the mother told me that she never wanted to see her husband again, and didn't want him to have any contact at all with the little girl. Furthermore, she was not asking him for any money, either for herself or the child, because she felt that that money would be stolen, and she wished to have no part of it. Her parents would help her and she would be able to manage without any help from him at all.

I thought that there might be some disagreement over her attitude, particularly over access to the child, but when I visited him in Wandsworth prison I found that this was not so. He told me that he never wanted to see his wife or child again. He would be prepared to send them some money, but as it will be stolen money, he knew that she would not accept it.

This puzzled me; I asked him if this meant that he intended to commit further offences, after his release?

'When I did my national service they put me into the Royal Engineers. They showed me how to use gelignite and I became a "jelly" expert. When I was demobbed I met some mates who were planning a robbery, and they paid me £500 to blow a safe for them. This was "clean" money. I was paid the £500 before the robbery, on the understanding that I received no more money, whatever was in the safe. I got nothing out of the robbery whatever, but when we got caught I still had my £500, which the police could not touch. They're waiting for me to come out now. We've got a bigger one planned, and I shall get about £1,000, just for blowing the safe.'

The welfare report for the Divorce Court presented no problems. But in preparing it, I had news of a possible future robbery. I felt dutybound to report these facts to the police, for whatever action they might feel to be appropriate.

There was another occasion when I was supervising a young schoolboy who was subject of a juvenile court supervision order. He had not committed a very serious offence, but he did not seem to me to be getting very much support or encouragement from his parents. His father was a self-employed builder and his mother had quite enough to do in running the rambling old house in which they lived. In order to supplement the family income, however, they did have two lodgers, and their son seemed, almost to be treated as a third. I thought that I might try and make the parents aware that a greater interest in the boy's work and play might bring the family closer together, to their mutual benefit. For several months I had encouraged this, but not with any dynamic results.

Then, one day, mother phoned and asked me to call round at once. It was most urgent. When I arrived, we sat in the sitting room and she surprised me by telling me that she was going to divorce her husband.

There followed a sad tale which I had had no reason ever to suspect. She said that she and her husband had really been living separate lives for several years. He was, she said, sexually disoriented and he would bring young men home with him from the pub, and then leave them with her in the hope that they would make advances towards her. She admitted that she had gone along with this to some extent, until she had discovered that he had knocked a hole through the wall, and could actually sit in an adjacent shed outside and watch what was going on. Inside the sitting room there was a pegboard in the recess painted pink, but it was there to conceal the hole in the wall.

Now, she said, there was something that she wanted me to see. We went outside the house into the side passage, by the back gate. The chimney was built to go right up the side of the house serving three rooms. At the bottom of the chimney, a small door had been built, and I was amazed to find that this door led into the front room fire grate. Inside the room, the old fashioned mantelpiece had been covered over with pegboard.

The room was 'let' to a young lady lodger, and she had been encouraged by the husband to entertain boyfriends whenever she liked. He was obviously getting into the fireplace by the outside door, in order to act as a Peeping Tom.

Let us pause a moment to consider the position in which I now found myself. My official position in relation to this family was that of supervising probation officer, attached to Wandsworth Juvenile Court. As such, my official client is the lad who is subject of the supervision order. But in his interests, the best results may be obtained by family casework. It is almost impossible to supervise a juvenile without involving the parents at some stage or other, and in varying degrees. It now seemed that the family situation was about to disintegrate, and although I was sympathetic toward the mother, it was the lad's future welfare that caused me most concern. I saw a lot of him in the next few weeks, and of course it emerged that he had known what was going on. I think I was able to help him considerably in the long run. But that is not the point I am stressing.

I contacted his father because I felt that the present situation could not be allowed to continue, and as a result of our discussion, the door in the chimney was removed, and the chimney was bricked up again.

Later, I received a letter from a solicitor informing me that a divorce hearing had been scheduled at the Royal Courts of Justice, and that I would be required as a witness. I was the only person, apart from the wife, who had actually seen the door in the chimney.

I was still supervising the boy in an official capacity, and whatever else may be said, the parties in this divorce case were still his parents. I informed the solicitor that the only way in which I was prepared to give evidence was under a witness summons. At least this may go a little way towards me preserving my neutrality. When I went into the witness box at the Royal Courts of Justice, I informed the judge that there is a Home Office directive that information come by in a privileged position, is subject to his ruling, and if I felt that by giving information I was abusing a position of trust, he could permit me not to do so. In fact the matter did not arise, and I was obliged to reveal what I had seen.

The point is, that had I not been a probation officer, on official duty, I would never have seen it at all. I had every sympathy for the parents, in differing ways, but my prime consideration (and my official consideration), had to be my own client.

Before leaving the subject of divorce welfare, there was one other case that serves to illustrate the problems that may have to be faced by the welfare officer, who, in spite of making every effort, fails to please everybody.

A lady colleague asked me if I would take over the case, because the father of two children, was behaving in a 'difficult' manner. When I first met him I realized that he was a very intelligent, but somewhat eccentric, man. His mode of dress resembled a garden gnome, with brightly coloured shirt, trousers, shoes, etc.

There had been a divorce, and he was given access to his two children, a boy aged ten years, and a girl aged eleven years. The parents lived in two separate houses in the same road, so that there was very little difficulty in them meeting, and mother didn't mind how often the children went to see their father. Only, they didn't want to go!

Now this gentleman decided that, as there was an order of the court granting him access, it was up to the welfare officer to ensure that it was carried out.

This is, in fact, not the case. In order to try and be helpful, however, I did have an interview with the two children, and I found them to be both bright and vociferous. They had decided ideas about what they intended to do, and sadly, their father did not enter into them. He was a strange man, and I could not blame the children for not wanting to have close contact with him. I still felt it was sad, however, here was a perfect example of the children dictating the play, in spite of the order of the court.

'He never wants to take us to the pictures or anywhere interesting. He takes us *where he wants to go*. To museums and places like that. We go to see him every Saturday morning because he's got our rabbits – if it wasn't for that, we wouldn't go at all!'

I tried to reason with them. 'After all, he is your father, and I'm sure that he is fond of you both.'

And then, out of the mouths of babes: 'He left us – we didn't leave him!'

☆ ☆ ☆

But there are many lighter moments in court too . . .

Jack Dunphy was the senior probation officer at the Inner London Quarter Sessions. There were three courts in action, and the three 'resident' judges were: Their Honours Mr R. Seaton, Mr F. Cassells, and Mr H. Elam.

Jack Dunphy was also a Football League referee, and one day, during the lunch-hour, Jack was asked to go to the Judges' retiring room. Wondering what it was all about, Jack duly arrived, knocked at the door, and entered apprehensively.

'Ah, Mr Dunphy,' said Mr Henry Elam. 'I wonder if you can help us? We have been trying to name the Spurs team of 1923, and we have got the whole team except the outside right – can you remember who that was?'

The name was on the tip of Jack's tongue, but at that moment, he just could not remember it.

'Now look here, Dunphy,' said Mr Elam. 'This will worry me all afternoon. If you remember it, you must let me know at once.'

Jack promised to do so, and went away, thinking hard about

the player in question.

During the afternoon he suddenly remembered who it was. He wrote the player's name on a piece of paper, and then went into Number Two Court, where Mr Elam was trying a case. A barrister was on his feet addressing the court, so Jack stood at the back and, upon catching the Judge's eye, waved his piece of paper. The Judge immediately told the barrister: 'I'm afraid I will have to stop you for a moment. Mr Dunphy has a most important message for me – come forward please Mr Dunphy.'

The barrister bowed to the Judge and sat down – the Clerk of the Court rose, turned and faced the Judge and bowed. Jack Dunphy went before the Clerk, bowed, and handed him his note. The Clerk turned to the Judge, bowed, and handed him the note.

The Judge read the note and beamed: 'Thank you, Mr Dunphy. I'm sure you are right. That was most important.'

Jack bowed and retired.

The barrister rose and continued his case . . . Spurs, outside right, 1923!

☆　☆　☆

During a case at the magistrates court, a police sergeant entered the witness box to give evidence against a defendant charged with assaulting the police. The defendant had, during a struggle in the police station, kicked the police sergeant in the ear, as he lay on the ground.

As if to prove this, the sergeant had a giant pad stuck upon his left ear with sticking plaster. I was sitting at the probation officer's table, rather bored, so I took out a piece of paper, and drew the sergeant with his ear bandaged and underneath I wrote: 'Wot's all this 'ere'.

I passed this across to the court police inspector, who stifled a grin, and passed it along the police bench, bringing grins to the faces of various officers.

On that day there were five J.P.s sitting on the bench, and as the paper was passed back to me, I noticed that the magistrate on the end had been watching what was going on. He (who shall be nameless) signalled to me to let him see the paper. I went quickly round the outside of the court and handed it up to the magistrate. He grinned, and then to my horror, passed it to the next magistrate. While this poor sergeant was giving evidence, my drawing went right along the bench, and back! Later, after I had retrieved it, the court inspector presented it to the sergeant, who luckily had a good sense of humour.

I got a wigging from the clerk!

☆ ☆ ☆

We had a gentleman in court one day who had pleaded guilty to indecent exposure. The Chairman of the Bench, also a gentleman, fined him £50. The man asked the Chairman if he could pay this fine weekly, and the Chairman asked him to give details of his income and expenditure. The man told the Chairman how much he earned, and then related a long list of payments that he was obliged to pay out each week. The Chairman thought about this for several minutes, and then said to the defendant: 'You haven't got a lot to play with, have you!'

☆ ☆ ☆

At the Old Bailey, the Common Sergeant, Sir Mervyn Griffith-Jones, once requested a report on a young man aged eighteen who had pleaded guilty to unlawful sexual intercourse with a girl aged fifteen, who was now pregnant by him.

I interviewed this young man at Ashford Remand Centre, and I was very surprised to discover that he already had two children by two women who were both much older than him. I was dutybound to include details of these children in my report, and I attended the hearing at the Old Bailey and presented the report myself.

Sir Mervyn was in his usual pleasant mood, until he read the report. By the time he had finished reading it I thought he was going to explode.

'Until I read the probation officer's report I was going to deal with you leniently . . . you can't go around getting women in the fam – er – family – er – family er er pregnant! You'll go to prison for six months!'

Not a perfect example of sentencing, but effective!

☆ ☆ ☆

His Honour Judge Frank Cassells was always my favourite judge. A man's man, he was always convivial and pleasant to work with. We once drank half a bottle of whisky between us at a reception, and when he left I pulled his leg by saying: 'Don't forget, next time I come to the Crown Court I will expect preferential treatment!'

Ever the Judge, he turned and solemnly told me: 'Everybody that comes to the Crown Court *gets* preferential treatment.'

He once put a man on probation, and said to me: 'Mr Mott, I'll get you to be a father to him.' Now as the man was only ten years younger than I was, I drew myself up to my full height in the witness box and said: 'I will treat him like a younger brother, Your Honour.'

He grinned and said: 'Hah – I wish I'd thought of that!'

☆   ☆   ☆

Unfortunately, confidentiality makes it impossible to relate the many acts of compassion and sympathy arrived at as being in the bests interests of justice. To the unenlightened, the appropriate course can sometimes be misconstrued as leniency. I never came across a case in which a defendant was treated leniently – in order to treat people equally you sometimes have to treat them unequally.

A young fellow came into court accused of stealing from the jackets of golfers, while they were playing golf and had left their clothes in the changing room.

It was revealed that he was a keen golfer himself and had at one time represented the county. He had purchased a set of golf clubs from the professional's shop, on the understanding that he paid weekly, but he had been unable to keep up the payments and had resorted to stealing in order to pay for the clubs. He pleaded guilty, and the magistrates retired to consider the case.

Now it so happened that the Clerk of the Court was a very keen golfer himself, but try as he may he had never been able to get his handicap down below twenty. While the magistrates were in retirement I went across to the dock to talk to the lad and put him at his ease. We talked about golf.

'What's your handicap?' I asked him.

'Seven,' he replied.

I could not resist the temptation of telling this to the Clerk of the Court.

'Do you know what his handicap is, sir?'

'No.'

'Seven.'

'The little bastard ought to be in Borstal!'

11

BROADMOOR

Usually referred to as 'Broadmoor', it is in fact Broadmoor Hospital, and the patients are extremely disturbed people who have committed serious offences, but were found to be suffering from mental illness. In such cases it is felt that confinement in a special hospital is more appropriate than imprisonment, and indeed, some of the patients do respond to treatment and are eventually released.

It is part of the job of the probation service to supervise such patients on licence, and a great deal of preparation and care is exercised both prior to, and after, release. Unfortunately, a great deal of adverse publicity is given to the very few cases that offend again, but because of the confidentiality extended to each of them, it is not possible to publicize the vast majority of cases which are successful. Of course, the public must be protected and every precaution is taken before a patient is finally released.

The supervising probation officer is certain to be an officer of experience, but this special type of supervision can be very demanding and is never taken lightly.

I have been to Broadmoor on only four occasions. The first of these was a visit of observation with a group of probation officers, who were expecting to become involved with patients on licence at a later date. I think that Broadmoor is a marvellous hospital that copes with the most difficult patients in an almost perfect manner. The workshops are highly efficient, and patients work in them with excellent results. They are encouraged to develop skills both in working and in leisure hours; they are encouraged in hobbies, they have a music room, and publish their own magazine which contains personal contributions.

I did feel rather sad when I saw a little old lady, in her room, with several budgerigars flying about out of their cage. I couldn't help feeling that there is so little difference between them and her. The staff are dedicated people doing a most difficult job in a most efficient way.

One amusing incident did occur while we were on this visit.

One of the visiting probation officers was my friend and colleague, Geoffrey Parkinson. Now Geoffrey is something of a character himself, but an excellent officer, with a great sense of humour, so I make no apology for my action.

The group arrived at an isolated building, and the person showing us round stopped outside and told us: 'This is the refractory wing. The patients in here are sometimes a bit aggressive. You do not have to come in if you prefer not to, but if you do, keep together and be on your guard.'

Of course, we all decided to enter, and I found it most interesting. So interesting in fact that I was lingering slightly behind the others, when a side door burst open, and a patient came up and grabbed me by my coat lapels.

'Are you the Home Secretary?' he asked aggressively, shaking my lapels.

Startled. I just replied: 'No.'

'Are you the Home Secretary?' he asked again. 'I am innocent. Are you the Home Secretary?'

At this point I looked over the poor chap's shoulder, and saw Geoffrey Parkinson standing about ten yards up the passage.

'You see that man standing there?' I said. 'Well, he's the Home Secretary!'

Luckily, for Geoffrey, the poor patient was intercepted before he could get his hands on him. I don't think he ever knew about that!

☆   ☆   ☆

On the next two occasions that I went to Broadmoor, I had organized a party from Rotary International, who were possibly prospective future employers. They had expressed willingness, in conjunction with the supervising officer, and the hospital social workers, to provide suitable employment for some of those released on licence. They were both, to some extent, educational visits, but they were worthwhile, and I know of at least one patient who had a job to go to on release.

I was sitting in my office one day, when the telephone rang.

'Mr Mott? I have the Home Office for you.'

What was all this about?

A Home Office official came to the phone and told me:

'The Principal Probation officer for Inner London has given us your name. It is a special job that we would like you to carry out at Broadmoor Hospital. There is a patient who has been in there for the past seven years, having committed a murder. At the time of his sentence, he threatened that when he came out he intended to murder his probation officer. The doctor at Broadmoor is now recommending his release – to a local mental hospital in the first instance – and later upon licence. The Home Secretary has requested that he should first be confronted by a probation officer, to study his reaction, and with regard to his suitability for release.

'It has been suggested that you may be a suitable officer for this special assignment!'

I think he thought he was doing me a favour!

I asked him: 'What about the officer doing it, that he threatened to kill – we'd know for sure then!'

'Sorry, but they think that's too risky.'

I duly arrived at Broadmoor, armed with all the documents of the case. The man in question had stabbed two youths in a cinema, and one of them had died. He had run home and barricaded himself in the flat, where he lived with his father. When his father attempted to let the police in, he hit him over the head with a chair. The probation officer had provided reports for the court, which recommended psychiatric reports from two doctors. As a result of such reports, a hospital order was made.

I went into the Centre, and was shown to a table, where our interview would take place. There were only two other visitors present. A man and a woman at the next table. My client was brought to me by a nurse, who stood by, not too far away. If Alfred Hitchcock had cast my client for his role, he could not have done better. Tall, pale, thin, hollow cheeked and staring eyes . . .

We shook hands.

'Would you like some tea?' (on sale at the counter).

I got the tea and he said: 'You are the first visitor I've ever

138

had!' . . . in seven years!

'Do you know who I am?'

'No.'

I watched him closely. 'I am a probation officer.'

'Ah, then I know why you have come.'

'Why do you think?'

'Because I threatened to kill my probation officer.'

He remembered his name, too.

I explained that this was, in fact, why I was here. I told him that he was being considered for release, and although I could not guarantee that it would happen, I could at least make a recommendation, but first I must know how he felt now.

He spoke quite reasonably. 'I don't want to kill him now. I just want to get out of here, get a room, and find a job. I won't be in any more trouble.'

We chatted for about half an hour. I was not qualified to comment on his medical condition, but he seemed rational and friendly. We said goodbye, and the nurse came over and escorted him away. Only then did the man and woman at the next table stand up.

'We are members of staff. We were here for your protection. Everybody here thought he would attack you!'

Some years later I had occasion to contact Broadmoor on another matter and I enquired about him. He was no longer in the hospital having been released some time ago. His probation officer is still alive and kicking, and, as luck would have it – so am I.

☆   ☆   ☆

Many of our clients are relieved at the thought of being placed on probation, and respond to supervision extremely well. Apart from the possible therapeutic value which may emerge from a casework situation, there is also a period of self-discipline, in keeping with the terms and conditions of the Probation Order. No doubt there are some of our clients who might offend again, without the support of a probation officer, but while success sometimes comes in unexpected cases, so too, extremely difficult cases may be uncovered. The probation service deals with a variety of different personalities, who have many problems that often relate to their character and development. A number of them can be aggressive and sometimes violent, and their behaviour can range from obstinacy, aggression and defiance, to threats and sometimes assaults.

It is essential that, in cases where there is a history of violence, the senior probation officer will ensure that the officer assigned to that case has the appropriate skills and experience, to deal with any emergency. This is not only for the protection of the public, but also in the interest of the officers and staff in the probation office.

After I had left the South Western office, an ex-client went there and demanded to see me. When he was told that I was no longer there, he started to smash up the chairs in the waiting room in frustration. I spoke to him on the telephone and got him to accept the fact that he should consult another officer. There was no danger to the officer – it was purely lack of self-control. It is usually easier to supervise possibly dangerous clients, when their previous history is known to you. But this cannot always be the case. A lady colleague was asked to prepare a report on a young man who was a first offender. She made an appointment to see him at her office one evening after he had finished work. This is not unusual, but it can mean that that officer is alone in the office, as she was on this occasion. This young man was obviously not taking the interview very seriously (a great mistake, this, for some of my female colleagues can be tougher than the men). When rebuked, he became aggressive, and picked up a paperknife which she foolishly had on top of her desk. He twisted her arm and actually drew a speck of blood with the point of the knife.

At the adjourned hearing she produced a report which, quite rightly, did not refer to this incident, because the report dealt only with a case in which he had already been found guilty. She did, however, state that he was unsuitable for probation.

I do not know if the magistrates became aware of the reason for this or not, but I have my suspicions. This young man was sentenced to six months' imprisonment. He could hardly complain.

☆   ☆   ☆

My desk was in the corner of my office, and I used to sit in the corner, behind it.

One day my door was slammed open and a man rushed in and came right up to the front of my desk. His eyes were blazing and he was obviously extremely disturbed. He was already subject of a probation order for threatening passers-by with a milk bottle. He was an ex-mental patient, and there was a condition in his probation order that he underwent psychiatric treatment.

I knew therefore that he could be aggressive and possibly violent. As he stood there, with eyes blazing, I knew that if I moved he would come over the desk at me. I sat perfectly still, and looked at him. Neither of us said a word. It seemed to me to be a very long time before he suddenly turned and dashed out of the office. I thought that the spell had been broken, and I called to him, but he did not return.

Five minutes later, I received a telephone call from Lavender Hill Police Station. 'Do you know a man called John ——?'

'Yes, I do.'

'He has just punched eight windows out of a telephone box!'

That telephone box was obviously me, but I never did find out the reason for it. Poor John, eventually he returned to Cane Hill Hospital.

☆ ☆ ☆

Unbalanced behaviour is almost impossible to predict, and yet it is always a possible problem that may have to be dealt with, after it has occurred. It is usually unpleasant and unnerving, but incidents do sometimes occur. The probation officer or his office staff should never be averse to calling for police assistance if needed.

I know of one case where an ex-prisoner actually took out an open razor and cut his own throat in the probation office. Imagine the distress, not to mention chaos, that had to be dealt with on that occasion.

Yes, there have been occasions when probation officers have been assaulted or attacked, sometimes seriously. Happily, such incidents are very few indeed, considering the personalities of some of the clients with whom we associate. Irate clients sometimes resort to breaking windows or other petty damage, and one actually set fire to the curtains in the waiting room. Such clients do sometimes respond to supervision and learn not to behave in such a childish manner. They are not a real danger, but do tend to make life unpleasant. It would be a mistake, however, to underestimate the possibility of real danger, under certain circumstances.

I have already referred to one or two incidents where the consequences may have been more serious than was actually the case. The senior probation officer at Richmond Magistrates Court had the alarming experience of being held, almost as a hostage, in his own office, at knife-point. This was a major incident, and lasted for a considerable time before the assailant eventually relented and gave himself up. The police were called in, and there were genuine fears that this officer might be severely injured. Whatever the outcome, it is a harrowing experience, and serves to emphasis my point, that it is always as well to be a little bit cautious. If you've got a paperknife, keep it in your drawer!

☆ ☆ ☆

On 1 December 1978, probation officer Arthur Caiger, was at home with his family, when there was a ring at the front door bell. When Arthur went to the door, there was a young man there, and he threw a beaker of acid into Arthur's face. He was rushed to the hospital immediately. Both of his eyes were affected, and in spite of the skilful efforts of the doctors involved, Arthur became totally blind. He was comforted by his sincere belief in God, and he says that, as he lay in the hospital, not knowing whether or not he would lose his sight, he felt nearer to God than ever before.

The person who committed this ghastly offence was never apprehended, in spite of strenuous police activity to try and trace him.

Arthur will be totally blind for the rest of his life, purely as a result of his efforts to make the world a better place in which to live. The latter, for both the rest of us and for people like the person who threw the acid.

To me, he epitomises the whole probation service. He enjoyed his job, but he dedicated most of his life to the benefit and well-being of others. He has even found it in his heart, because of his strength and his religious beliefs, to forgive his attacker. Never forget Arthur Caiger. There, but for the grace of God, go the rest of us.

☆   ☆   ☆

In recent years there have been a number of changes within the probation service, some on a statutory basis, and some that are the result of the efforts of individual officers, with skills that they put to good use, in the interest of the client.

In almost every probation area there exists some project or other designed to assist in the rebuilding of character, and to help people to lead a better life.

Some years ago, as a result of the Wootton Report, Community Service Units were established. Community Service Orders were put into operation, mainly as an alternative to a custodial sentence. The Units were organized and run by the probation service, but in most areas it was found necessary to employ additional staff with the suitable ability to organize jobs for the clients.

A Community Service Order could not be made without the assurance that the client would be a suitable candidate, and that suitable work was available. The client would also have to consent to such an Order being made. These Units have grown considerably and to a large extent have grown away from the 'hard graft' type of work, which at its worst was only a form of punishment, with very little reformative value. At best, it provided a useful outlet, and allowed a client to remain at home, so that, at least, his family did not suffer from the adverse effects that may have resulted from a prison sentence. Today, the Units are well organized, and in addition to practical work, they have developed such things as day centres for the elderly, which are organized by the Units, but staffed, with supervision, by the clients. They organize outings for the disabled and are generally encouraged to take part in activities which are proving far more successful than the purely labouring type of work which was, at first, expected of them.

There are other projects that are organized by the Probation Service and staffed by probation officers, paid employees, and quite often, voluntary workers. These include such things as motor mechanics courses, where youngsters are encouraged to accept a more responsible role in society, in addition to acquiring genuine expertise.

Voluntary hostels, bail hostels, and lodgings schemes have developed on a large scale in the past few years, as more and more people seem to have problems of homelessness.

Female clients are, where possible, supervised by female officers, and special advice in things such as mothercare, are encouraged if appropriate.

The aims and objects of the probation service are geared toward the rehabilitation of its clients in the broadest sense. But practical assistance must sometimes take priority because it is not practical to try and assist with the solution of personal problems, where the overriding factor is lack of accommodation, work or money. The idea that heavy punishment will act as a deterrent, to persons under severe stress, is outdated, and certainly, in most cases, untrue. Encouragement and assistance, to cope with one's problems and become self-sufficient is far more likely to reduce minor offences.

The new ideas of tagging offenders with electronic devices in order to keep a check upon them, is surely a retrograde step, and an infringement of human rights. It seems to me to be nothing more than the modern version of the ball and chain.

The suggested imposition of curfews seems to be impractical and may cause more problems than it actually solves.

The supervising of such cases is not consistent with the philosophy that has set the guidelines of the probation service since the Probation of First Offenders Act in 1927. It is my belief, that the British judicial system is the finest in the world, and I am not sure that copying American methods can do anything to improve it.

In the probation service, this country has a first-class, highly trained organization, experienced in dealing with all types of offenders, in a variety of ways. The idea that probation is lenient treatment is nonsense. It is an effective method of reformation that, in a large number of cases, prevents a repetition of antisocial behaviour, that his hitherto led to offences being committed.

☆   ☆   ☆

This, then, is the story of my twenty-four years as a probation officer. The experiences that I have related here have been interesting, tragic, humorous and often rewarding. But most of all, educational, for as I have dealt with each case, I found that I too learned from the other person's experience. I hope that I have managed, in some small way, to pass this on.

On my last day at the office, I was somewhat sadly packing up, when my door opened, and in came ex-Commando Bill. He was a tough cookie, as were other members of his family, whom I had helped from time to time.

'I've just come to say goodbye, Mr Mott, and to thank you for all you've done for me and my family.'

He came across the room and we shook hands. As he left, he turned in the doorway, and said: 'Don't forget – if ever you want anyone done over . . .!'

POSTSCRIPT

In 1978 a Home Office Inspector arrived at my office. He pointed out that the parole system had now been in operation for ten years, and he had been commissioned to inspect all parole cases, going back ten years. It is usual to keep files for ten years from the last entry, so I was in a position to supply him with the case histories of all my parole cases over that period. There were quite a number, but perhaps not as many as would be the case in a busier area.

He took them to an empty office and began to check them.

In the afternoon, he came back to my office, and said he would like to take the files away for a few days to study them. He then said: 'I notice that you don't see all your parolees every week. The Home Office takes the view that these people are serving a prison sentence under your jurisdiction, and expects you to see them every week.'

'In giving me the privilege of supervising ex-prisoners, in the role of parole officer, I take the view that I also have the right to supervise them in my own way, and see them when I feel it to be necessary!'

He looked rather hostile. 'I can tell you now, that the Home Office will not back you if anything goes wrong, if you haven't seen them every week.'

He turned and left the office.

A few days later, he returned with all the files, and brought them to my office. we looked at each other, I thought a little oddly, and then: 'I don't know about not backing you. I think we should study your methods . . . In ten years, you've *never* had a failure!'

Six years later, when I left the probation service, I had still not had a parole failure.

SUCCESS
To laugh often and much; to win the respect of intelligent people, and the affection of children; to

earn the appreciation of honest critics, and endure the betrayal of false friends; to appreciate beauty, to find the best in others; to leave the world a bit better, whether by a healthy child, a garden patch, or a redeemed social condition; to know even one life has breathed easier because you lived. This is to have succeeded.

Ralph Waldo Emerson